BUNKERED

A comedy in two acts

Lynn Brittney

Published by Playstage
United Kingdom

An imprint of Write Publications Ltd

www.playsforadults.com

Designed by Kate Lowe, Greensands Graphics
Printed by Creeds Ltd, Bridport, Dorset

Note to producers staging "Bunkered"

This play is very easy to stage – having one fixed set, a central doorway and all the action taking place on the set or in the corridor at the back of the set. There are, however, a few sound effect and lighting effect requirements.

Firstly, there is a lot of turning on and off of lights and the stage, at times, only being lit by the battery-operated storm lamps on the set. There is a need for the two equipment screens to light up. Although these cannot be seen by the audience, they do need to see the lights from the screens reflected in the actor's faces. There is also a need for various sound effect offstage: sonar blips; a klaxon; a robotic voice; telephone conversations and a metal door clanging shut and opening. All of these can be downloaded from the internet (except the telephone conversations) from a site such as www.sound-effects-library.com.

It is suggested that the set is reminiscent of a military bunker and, to that end, we have provided a photo of a similar facility at the back of the book. The posters suggested are The British Navy Guards The Freedom of Us All and Keep Calm and Carry On – both of which can be sourced at the Imperial War Museum website or shop. Admiralty Charts are, usually, very expensive but you can pick up replicas (only one would be needed and it wouldn't matter which one) on Ebay for a modest amount.

Accurate naval uniforms are obviously required. MAGS and JOAN would be wearing WRNS uniforms (old issue), whilst PETER's uniform is several sizes too small. Commodore SHELTON needs to wear an up to date uniform for a serving woman officer. The Marines need to be in camouflage combat gear, with helmets, gloves and guns. If your local costume source cannot oblige, then try a website such as www.thehistorybunker.co.uk.

The characters in the play are pretty much encapsulated in the text and action. JOAN is the senior officer and very organised, MAGS is a bit feather-brained and likes needlework, PETER is a bit of a fusspot. Sub-Lieutenant CONNOR is a highly trained, but highly strung, Marine Commando. Midshipman TAYLOR is a surprisingly competent young woman. HARRY, the anarchist, is one of life's oddballs; BILL is obsessed with his pigeons, whilst Commodore SHELTON is a tough woman who has worked her way up in the Royal Navy and is hanging on by her fingertips.

Just a note about the voices offstage, these take the form of Admiralty telephone conversations and a BBC news announcement. We do say in the cast list that the voices could be male or female but we would add that, for the sake of credibility, they should not all be female. A mix would be preferable. The voices should be recorded, to give that sound of happening 'elsewhere'.

The action is gentle comedy punctuated with manic bursts of farce. Don't lose the pace during the gentle moments but don't speak over the laughs from the audience!

BUNKERED

CAST *(In order of appearance)*

PETER   Aged 64. He is a conscientious worrier. Takes his job very seriously.

HARRY   Aged 60. An eternal hippy. Obssessed with aliens and conspiracy theories. Very good handyman.

JOAN   Harry's sister. Peter's senior officer. Very practical. In her early 60s. The organiser of the group. Loves the Navy.

MAGS   Joan's friend and co-worker. In her late fifties. A bit disorganised. Married to the absent BILL.

CONNOR   A very 'gung'ho' Marine in his late thirties.

TAYLOR   A rather competent girl in her late teens/early twenties.

BILL   Aged 65. Stayed at home with 'man flu'. Loves looking after his pigeons.

COMMODORE
SHELTON   Tough but fair Navy career woman, aged 60.

VOICE 1   (offstage, recorded) Could be male or female.

VOICE 2   (offstage, recorded) Could be male or female.

BBC Announcer (offstage, recorded) Could be male or female.

4 men, 4 women and 3 voices offstage.

The action of the play takes place in the operations room of an abandoned Cold War Naval Intelligence Bunker somewhere in the United Kingdom.

BUNKERED

ACT I

SCENE I

Stage is dark. Suggested music "Theme from the Ipcress File" to create atmosphere of Cold War spying. Music fades. The door opens, throwing a shaft of light on to the stage. In the doorway is HARRY, who is blindfolded, and PETER, who switches on the light in the room to reveal the operations centre of the Naval Intelligence bunker. PETER is carrying HARRY's toolbox. The screens of the equipment (radar/sonar etc.) are facing upstage and cannot be seen by the audience. There are four chairs dotted about and a small table to one side, which has a thick document underneath one leg of the table. The walls are painted Battleship Grey and there are various Government posters on the wall and an Admiralty chart of coastal waters. (SEE SET PLAN/PHOTO AT THE END OF THE PLAY AND ALSO PRODUCER'S NOTES.)

HARRY	Are we finally here? I mean we must have come down loads of corridors and stuff. We must be here by now.
PETER	Yes, yes. We're finally here. You can take your blindfold off now.
	(HARRY takes his blindfold off and beams with delight.)
HARRY	Unbelievable! Just unbelievable!
PETER	*(smiling)* I thought you'd be impressed. Sorry about all the blindfold business, Harry, but this place is top secret – you understand.
HARRY	Oh think nothing of it, mate. Gawd, that was a journey! And I know we're near the sea because I could hear the seagulls. It was like that film – you know – Whatsitsname – where the bloke tries to retrace his journey in a car to where he was kidnapped by blindfolding himself and listening to

all the sounds. That's what I was doing. *(He starts peering at all the instruments.)* Cor blimey! Look at this! It's an old sonar, isn't it? I haven't seen one of those in years! Can I... can I have a fiddle with it?

PETER   *(handing over the toolbox)* Be my guest, mate. That's what I brought you down here for. The electrical gubbins are underneath the monitors.

(HARRY opens up his toolbox and gets out a screwdriver and begins to open up the panels under the machines.)

HARRY   So, what's the story behind this place? I mean, you told me a bit of the background but I didn't really understand...

PETER   *(producing several sheets of paper from his pocket)* I'm afraid I'll have to get you to sign The Official Secrets Act first, Harry. I should have done it before but I didn't want to scare you off.

HARRY   *(straightening up in surprise)* Are you serious?

PETER   Absolutely!

HARRY   Pete...mate...I can't sign that form...it's against my religion!

PETER   What?

HARRY   I'm an anarchist. I can't sign a form that binds me to a fascist dictatorship and promises never to reveal its secrets. I would be betraying humanity!

PETER   What the hell are you talking about?

HARRY   I'm an anarchist.

PETER   Well I wish you'd told me before I brought you down here! I never would have asked you, if I'd known!

HARRY   Well, sorry, mate. But when you said you had a secret job for me to do, you should have said it was on behalf of the Government and then I would have said no. If the brotherhood knew that I'd signed that form they'd…well…I don't know what they'd do! At the very least they'd block my access to the Conspiracy Today weblog!

PETER   Well, I don't know what to do now. I've obviously picked totally the wrong bloke to do this job. I may have to kill you.

HARRY   *(alarmed)* What! Have you lost your marbles?

PETER   *(calmly)* No. It says in the Operations Manual that if an enemy infiltrates this facility, I have to kill them.

HARRY   *(holding up his screwdriver defensively)* Listen, don't start getting weird on me. You asked me to come to your workplace and repair some electrics. I didn't know that it was going to make you psychotic. I mean…I put up with all the blindfolding stuff, even though I did think it was a bit strange, but this is a joke too far. I mean…it's me, Pete. You've known me since I was a kid.

PETER   *(embarrassed)* I know, Harry. Look, I'm sorry, mate. I got a bit spooked when you wouldn't sign the form…I take my job too seriously, that's all.

HARRY   *(nodding)* OK. I can understand that – or, at least, I would understand that if I knew what this was all about…but I'm not signing any form. Right?

PETER   *(sighing)* OK. I'll try and explain…

(At this point JOAN comes in, carrying a pint of milk. She is wearing a Women's Royal Naval uniform. She doesn't see HARRY at first.)

JOAN   I stopped off the get some milk. We ran out yesterday and if

	I don't have my morning cup of tea, I get really scratchy. *(She spots HARRY.)* What's *he* doing here!?
PETER	*(anxious)* Now, don't get upset, Joan. It's only Harry.
JOAN	*(annoyed)* I know who he is, you pillock, he's my own brother!
PETER	I just felt we really had to sort out the electrics...
JOAN	*(exasperated)* So you chose Harry? My idiot brother?
HARRY	Oy!
JOAN	I'm sorry, Harry, but you are the last person I would invite into this facility – as you are a bone fide member of the Crackpot Club.
PETER	Oh come on...he's not that bad...
JOAN	Not that bad! This is my brother we're talking about, whose nickname at school was Loonybin, or have you forgotten? My mother's never lived down the metal biscuit tin episode.
PETER	The what?
HARRY	Oh trust you to bring that up.
JOAN	Harry, when you were seven you stole our biscuit tin, made a couple of eye holes in it, just so that you could go and have a conversation with next door's dog, because you were convinced that it was an alien mutation from outer space and you said the metal biscuit tin prevented your brains from getting fried!
HARRY	I was only seven...and anyway, it was a very strange animal, it was a mutation between a dog and a sheep. Tell me that's not strange!
JOAN	*(scornfully)* It was a Bedlington terrier! They look like little lambs!

PETER   Oh yes, I've seen those…

JOAN   *(warming to her subject)* And he sat there for an hour, with a biscuit tin on his head, trying to talk to the poor thing until the neighbours called the police. Then there was the time, when he was a teenager, he decided that the government were trying to drug us all by spraying the streets with mind-altering drugs.

PETER   And were they?

JOAN   Were they hell! It was a street cleaning lorry – you know, with the brushes by the wheels. And *this* is the person you choose to bring into a top secret Government facility. My idiot brother.

PETER   He's a very good electrician…very handy with machinery.

JOAN   Oh I know that. I remember the time he took my mother's washing machine apart and tried to build a satellite launcher.

PETER   Get away! *(To HARRY)* Did it work?

HARRY   *(enthusiastically)* Nearly! I couldn't quite get the trajectory right though.

JOAN   No. What happened was he shot a tin can into the next county. It's a miracle he didn't kill anyone.

PETER   What was it supposed to achieve?

HARRY   Well…I had a tape player on continuous loop inside the can – playing Edison Lighthouse…

JOAN   *(interrupting)* Yes. The policeman who found it was nearly driven berserk by continuous "Love grows where my Rosemary goes". He couldn't switch it off !

HARRY	No. That was because I'd built a self-generating power source in it so that if I had gotten it into space, it would have spread the love to all alien civilizations for all eternity.
PETER	*(convinced)* You are loony, aren't you?
HARRY	*(defensively)* I have a different perspective on life to most people, that's all. Anyway…what's this all about? This "top secret Government facility"? And what are you doing in uniform, Joanie?
JOAN	I'm a Second Officer in the Wrens – or at least I was, until they amalgamated with the Navy in 1993. I should be a Lieutenant now.
HARRY	*(disbelieving)* Get out of it! You've been in the Navy all these years and I didn't know about it? You told me you worked for the Inland Revenue!
JOAN	I never told you that. You *assumed* that's where I worked. I just told you I worked for the Government.
HARRY	Well, I did at one point, think you might be a spy…
JOAN	*(sarcastically)* You do surprise me.
HARRY	But then I discounted it because you always seemed to work nine to five and no spy would keep such regular hours. So, Pete, does that mean you work for the Navy as well?
PETER	Yes I do. I'm a Chief Petty Officer.
HARRY	Get away! Are you sure I'm the loony tunes around here?
JOAN	I'll have you know, Harry, that Peter and I – and two others – have been manning this Intelligence post since 1973.
HARRY	Well I never! So what is it that you do here, then?
PETER	That is top secret.

JOAN	Well…technically, it *was* top secret…
HARRY	Was?
JOAN	*(To PETER)* Well, you brought him down here! The cat's out of the bag now. You might as well tell him.
PETER	*(sighing)* They forgot about us.
HARRY	Pardon?
PETER	The Navy. They forgot about us. Look, they set up this bunker at the height of the Cold War…
HARRY	What…the old East versus West, Russia against America stuff?
PETER	Yes. We are…were…supposed to monitor the coastline to make sure that no unauthorised vessels – like Russian nuclear submarines – were coming inside the three mile limit. But then, suddenly, in 1991, the Cold War was officially over, so they decided to close down all the bunkers and make the personnel redundant.
JOAN	So we reported to Headquarters, only to find that they didn't have our names down anywhere and they told us to go away. We came back here and waited for someone to tell us what was happening…
PETER	Only they never did. Our paycheques kept coming and no-one ever contacted us again.
HARRY	So…let me get this right…you and your mates have been drawing Naval pay for the last, however many years…
JOAN	Twenty years.
HARRY	Twenty years…and coming into this bunker…and doing what?

PETER	*(uncomfortable)* Well…nothing…really. We didn't like to monitor the seaways or make any reports because we well…
JOAN	We didn't want to lose our jobs, basically. We've just kept quiet for the last twenty years. But, we've always come in every day and put on our uniforms, just in case the Navy suddenly pays a visit and then we could say that we assumed that we were supposed to carry on. *(To PETER)* Where is your uniform, by the way?
PETER	Oh! Sorry, Joan, I haven't had time to change. I'll go and do it now. *(PETER exits)*
HARRY	You jammy sods! You've been drawing full pay all this time and doing nothing for it!
JOAN	*(shrugging)* It's not our fault if the Navy couldn't get their computerised payroll right. But we've only taken our salaries – from which tax has been deducted at source, I may add. We haven't charged the Navy for our food or electricity.
HARRY	So how do you keep the place going then?
JOAN	It's got a diesel generator. Every month we have a whip round and buy the diesel to keep it going. We've tried to be as honest as we can. *(PETER re-appears, half wearing a uniform that is several sizes too small.)*
HARRY	You seriously need a new uniform, mate!
PETER	I know. It fitted me when I was twenty eight but I can't ask the Navy for a new one, can I?
JOAN	So what exactly was it that you brought Harry in to do – without my permission, by the way – and as I outrank you, I should put you on a charge.

PETER	Don't be daft, Joan. I brought Harry in to bring the equipment up to scratch.
JOAN	Why, for God's sake?
PETER	Because I shall be retiring soon...
JOAN	You don't know that.
PETER	Well I'm assuming that the Headquarter's computer will decide that I am sixty five and therefore should be pensioned off. At least I hope it does.
JOAN	I think you're assuming a lot, Peter. That computer could very well go on chugging out our paycheques forever, without any idea of our ages.
PETER	I know. I'm very worried about my pension.
HARRY	You may not get a pension, mate. You may have to just hope the paycheques keep on coming until you snuff it.
PETER	Thank you, Harry, I am aware of my own mortality.
JOAN	No, but Harry's right, Peter. None of us can assume that we are going to get a pension. Anyway, we've had this conversation before, with monotonous regularity. That's why we all pay in to the retirement fund. But I still don't understand why the equipment needs the tender care of my brother.
PETER	I just felt that if...if...I do get my retirement papers this year, I wanted to leave the equipment in the best possible working order. After all, as Chief Petty Officer, I am supposed to be responsible for the smooth running of this ship.
HARRY	Fine by me. As long as I don't have to sign any stupid Official Secrets Act, I would love to have a go at repairing

this equipment.

JOAN   I don't think we need bother with the Official Secrets Act.

HARRY   You tell him that! *(indicating PETER)* He was going to kill
                me as an enemy alien just before you came in.

JOAN   *(laughing)* I think you're safe there, Harry. Peter can't even
                kill a spider in the store cupboard.

                *(MAGS arrives. She is wearing her uniform and is struggling
                with a very large dress form which is dressed in a
                voluminous white wedding dress. She also has a bag over
                her shoulder, which has all her sewing things in.)*

MAGS   *(jolly)* Permission to come aboard, Joanie?

JOAN   *(giving her a hand)* Whatever have you got here, Mags?

MAGS   It's our Carol's wedding dress. I've got to get it finished by
                Saturday, so I've had to bring it in.

                *(They stand the dress form in the centre of the room and
                everyone looks at it.)*

PETER   I don't mean to be rude, Mags, but your niece is a big girl
                isn't she?

MAGS   *(nodding)* I know. Poor thing. It was all that hysteria over
                Wham in the eighties. She spent four years going to every
                concert, screaming her head off, and the doctor said that it
                damaged her adrenal glands, so the weight starting piling
                on. Then, when George Michael came out of the closet, she
                took to her bed with depression and ate doughnuts for a
                year. Ruined her life really. He's got a lot to answer for, that
                George Michael. *(brightening up)* Her mother – my sister –
                was the same. In fact it was the same sort of scenario, come
                to think of it. She had this lifelong crush on Richard

Chamberlain and had a nervous breakdown when he came out of the closet. Mind you she was going through the menopause at the time, so she might have had a nervous breakdown anyway. But it didn't help.

But Carol's had a new lease of life recently. She met a bloke through one of those internet dating sights and she's getting married at the age of thirty seven. That's why she's gone a bit over the top with the wedding dress. It would have looked nice on Carol when she was twenty but it's not really what I would have chosen now she's close on forty.

JOAN   No. Still those puff sleeves will hide her bingo wings, won't they?

MAGS   There's that I suppose.

HARRY   Sorry to interrupt this fashion statement moment but could you show me what you want me to do.

MAGS   *(noticing HARRY for the first time)* Oh hallo Harry! I didn't see you there! Been on any good protest marches lately?

HARRY   No. I couldn't go to the G20 summit one 'cos the dog had pups.

MAGS   Oh that's nice! How many?

HARRY   Seven.

PETER   Yes, if you come over here, Harry, I'll explain this scanner here.

HARRY   Have you got a manual?

PETER   Yes. In this drawer here.

(He opens a drawer and takes a file out. HARRY leafs through it. JOAN and MAGS busy themselves with the finer points of the wedding dress.)

HARRY	Cor blimey! It's a Japanese scanner! Bloody marvellous isn't it. They lose World War Two and then get rich making all our equipment for the Cold War. Bloody capitalist economics! Drives me to distraction! *(He finishes taking the panel off.)* Ah, yes. Here's your problem. Two of the wires have corroded. Have you got any wire and stuff in this place?
PETER	We have a very well-equipped storeroom as a matter of fact. Just follow me. Joan! Just taking Harry to the storeroom. Can I have the keys, please?
	(JOAN nods and takes a bunch of keys off her belt. PETER and HARRY exit.)
MAGS	So you decided to let Harry in on the secret, did you?
JOAN	Nothing to do with me, Mags. Peter got it into his head that we needed to get the equipment up to scratch before he retired. He didn't even discuss it with me. I should be very cross but I can't be bothered. Where's Bill, by the way?
MAGS	He's got man-flu. Asked me to sign him off sick.
JOAN	Oh. *(She goes to a desk drawer and takes out a book and makes some notes.)* That's a bugger. It means that one of us will have to do the pigeons today. I hate doing the pigeons.
MAGS	Oh Pete will do it. He doesn't mind.
	(PETER and HARRY re-enter. HARRY is carrying a roll of electrical wire.)
PETER	*(overhearing)* What won't I mind?
JOAN	Doing the pigeons. Bill's got man-flu.
PETER	Ooh nasty. Don't worry. I will do the pigeons. No problem.

HARRY	Pigeons? *(Hopefully)* Is that a code word for some weapons system?
PETER	No mate. They're pigeons. You know…birds. Royal Naval carrier pigeons…to be used in the event of a lockdown.
HARRY	How does that work then?
JOAN	Well, up there…*(She points to the ceiling.)* there is a small pigeon loft, with a very small opening into the outside world. The idea was, that if we were invaded by the Russians, the facility would lock down so that no-one could get in or out and, if the communications were cut off, we could release a pigeon, carrying a message, from the loft and it would go straight to Admiralty headquarters.
MAGS	Or, as is the case now, my home.
HARRY	Why your home?
PETER	Because her husband, Bill, is in charge of the pigeons and he trained this latest generation of birds to go to his house, instead of Admiralty HQ.
MAGS	Mind you, that's not a lot of good, really, when we're both here every day.
JOAN	No, but we couldn't carry on training them to go to the Admiralty, could we? Talk sense. We're not supposed to be here.
MAGS	True.
JOAN	The point is that we kept up with the breeding and training of the pigeons, so if the Admiralty did find out we were here, we are seen to be doing what we were paid to do.
PETER	See! That's my point entirely! That's why we need to get the equipment sorted out. With both Bill and me coming up to

retirement age, there's a very strong chance they could discover the mistake they made with the payroll. We need to have everything in working order.

JOAN   *(sighing)* I suppose so. Carry on then.

(HARRY beams with delight and starts taking off another panel. JOAN gets rubber gloves and a spray cleaner out of her bag and makes for the door.)

I'm just going to clean the officer's toilets. Mags, did you bring the lunch?

MAGS   I did. I made a cottage pie with veg. I left it in the galley to thaw. There should be enough for Harry, seeing as Bill isn't here.

HARRY   *(bobbing his head up)* What, you have hot lunches and everything, then? I may have to spin out this job a bit longer!

JOAN   Actually, now Pete has roped you in, we might as well get you to do a few other jobs as well. That toilet in number two head is not working again and the oven in the galley needs a bit of a going over.

MAGS   Oh, and the light fitting in the store cupboard keeps going on the blink...

HARRY   *(cheerfully)* Oh I could still be here at Christmas then! Is there an office party?

PETER   Well, we do put up a few decorations and break out the mulled wine...

HARRY   Excellent.

JOAN   Right, well I'm off to do a bit of cleaning.

MAGS   I'll be along in a minute, Joanie, I just want to get this sleeve
              sewn up.

JOAN   No hurry.

              *(JOAN exits, MAGS threads a needle and starts sewing one
              of the sleeves of the bridal dress. HARRY starts cutting off
              some pieces of wire from the bale and stripping the ends.)*

HARRY   D'you know, I still can't get over the fact that my own sister
              has been working in this place for god-knows-how-many
              years and kept it a secret.

PETER   Well, that's what you do when you work for the
              Government. Secrecy is part of the game.

HARRY   *(distracted from his work)* And that just goes to prove my
              theory about 9/11.

MAGS   Come again?

HARRY   Well, those of us who think that 9/11 was a neo-con
              government conspiracy – and there are many of us – are
              constantly told by sceptics that it would have taken a great
              many people to pull off a stunt like that and all those people
              wouldn't have been able to keep such a thing secret. But you
              lot are living proof that people working for a government
              are able to keep secrets for a very, very long time.

PETER   I suppose that's true.

HARRY   Of course it is, mate! Think of all those people who worked
              for Bletchley Park during the war. They all kept it a secret,
              didn't they? Until the government released some of the
              papers…and then they could talk about it. Mind you…this
              situation here…in this bunker is also showing the other side
              of the coin as well.

MAGS	Meaning?
HARRY	Government incompetence, Mags, government incompetence!
PETER	Now, hang on a minute…
HARRY	No. You can't defend that observation, Pete. You three… well, four, counting Bill…have been here, on full pay, due to government incompetence. That's fair isn't it?
MAGS	He's got you there, Pete. You can't deny that we owe our livelihoods to a cock-up by the Royal Navy.
PETER	Well…yes…but…
HARRY	No. There's no defence. Government incompetence. It's the scourge of our lives nowadays. Made even worse by the fascists in Brussels.
PETER	But the Navy wouldn't have been…at fault…if we had properly owned up and sorted it all out in. It's our fault really.
HARRY	I'm just going to take another panel off and see how much wire I'm going to need. Hold those bits for me will you, mate. *(HARRY hands PETER several bits of prepared wire and takes a third panel off.)* Yep. It looks like the wires are corroded in everything. *(HARRY starts cutting some more wire and returns to his political discourse.)* I mean, you say it's your fault…
PETER	What?
HARRY	Being here on full pay and what have you…
PETER	Oh we're back on that are we?

HARRY	But it's not your fault. The government can't have it both ways. It trains people up to be secretive and then it can't expect you to abandon all that training and 'sort things out' as you put it. Can it?
PETER	*(becoming confused by HARRY's logic)* No I suppose not. I mean we did try...
MAGS	He did. Pete and Bill went up to the Admiralty twice and tried to find out whether we'd been allocated other jobs or we were to be made redundant. Joanie should have gone really, being the senior ranker – but she was too upset.
HARRY	So what happened?
PETER	Well the first time we saw this Commander, who took a few notes and said he'd sort it out. Then we waited for a few months and there was no word, so we went again and saw a different bloke – some Sub-Lieutenant – who also took a few notes and said he'd sort it out. Then we waited and waited...but nothing happened.
HARRY	My point exactly. Government incompetence.
PETER	Well it was a very difficult time for the Navy. The Cold War was officially over – Glasnost and all that – and the Armed Services were being restructured. We just got lost in the midst of all that.
HARRY	But supposing you'd been trained as killers, eh?
PETER	What, me?!
HARRY	Yeah, it happens all the time in America. The government trains people as killers then makes them redundant or gets them to fight a pointless war that leaves them feeling useless and then they go all 'postal' and go on the rampage with an automatic machine gun in some shopping mall.

MAGS	*(laughing)* I can't imagine Pete going on a rampage anywhere!
HARRY	Ah, you may laugh, but it happens. Governments have a habit of using and discarding useful people and it can send them crazy. Any chance of a cup of tea?
	(Just then JOAN enters with a tray of tea and biscuits.)
	Look at that! She must have read my mind!
JOAN	No, I did not. No-one – not even the greatest psychic on the planet – could read your bizarre thoughts, Harry. I just realised that I was gasping for my morning cuppa and decided to leave the cleaning until later. *(She puts the tray on the nearest worktop.)* Tea up then!
HARRY	*(grabbing the nearest cup and ladling a great deal of sugar into it)* What no ration of rum? I thought the Navy always had rum in their tea?
JOAN	What do you think this is? The Battle of Trafalgar? You'll have to make do with biscuits. Without weevils and from the supermarket. Just like the modern Navy.
HARRY	I'm glad you made the tea because I'm going to have to turn the power off in a minute.
PETER	Oh right. I'd better break out the storm lamps. *(PETER goes to a cupboard and gets out three battery operated storm lamps and switches them on. Then he dots them around the room.)*
HARRY	*(putting down his tea)* Where's the power switch?
PETER	It's outside, in corridor three. Follow me.
	(PETER picks up one of the storm lamps and exits, followed by HARRY.)

MAGS *(getting a cup of tea and moving a chair to centre stage)* Well, this makes a change, doesn't it Joanie?

JOAN *(drawing up another chair next to MAGS)* Yeah. A bit of relief from the tedium. You can always count on our Harry to liven things up a bit.

MAGS He's harmless really. Good natured and all. *(The lights go out and the stage is lit only by the storm lamps.)* Oops! Here we go!

(PETER and HARRY come back through the door. HARRY immediately goes over to the equipment and starts work, occasionally stopping to slurp his tea. PETER draws up a chair next to JOAN and they all sit drinking their tea in the gloom.)

PETER I shall be able to sleep at night now, knowing that my equipment is all in working order.

MAGS *(giggling)* I hope you're talking about the equipment in this room!

PETER Eh? *(Then getting the joke.)* Oh! You daft woman!

JOAN At least when you retire, you won't be taking this lot home with you. Bill has announced his intention of taking all the pigeons home when he retires.

MAGS *(irritated)* Yes...aren't I the lucky one?

HARRY *(from behind the machinery)* So, when Bill and Pete retire, are you two girls going to carry on coming in here every day?

MAGS Well, we don't know really...

JOAN The trouble is, I'll still have five years to go before I draw a pension...and, I'm not sure what I would do with myself if I didn't come in here every day.

MAGS	Me too. I mean, I love Bill dearly...it's our silver wedding in three month's time...but I'm not too sure about spending all day and every day at home with him. At least here, there are other people to talk to.
HARRY	*(popping up for a slurp of tea)* Dear God! You can always go out, you know! Join clubs – go on a cruise – loads of things! I can see that you lot have become institutionalised, like all the other Government employees. Like those sad old gits who've spent their life in the Army and are lost when they come out.
JOAN	*(annoyed)* Oy! Who are you calling a sad old git?! At least I don't spend my life going to meetings of the local Anarchist's Society, pretending that I'm some bloody radical student who's going to change the world! Some of us have bothered to grow up, Harry...take responsibility for ourselves and our country.
HARRY	*(from behind the machinery again)* Alright, alright. Don't get on your soapbox, Joanie. Gawd help us! We're still having the same arguments we had when we were teenagers! *(He stands up.)* There! That should do it! For two of them, anyway. Do you want to put the power back on, Pete?
PETER	Will do. *(PETER exits with a storm lamp. Within a few seconds the lights come back on and everyone jumps up as one of the scanners lights up and starts beeping. What they don't notice is that a red light, which is hidden from their view, is flashing. They cluster round the scanner, their faces bathed in an orange glow. PETER switches off the storm lamps.)*
HARRY	What's happening then? It's not the Russians invading is it?
JOAN	*(scornfully)* No! I'm not sure exactly. The sonar is picking

up a submarine just off the coast.

PETER   Oh, I know what that is! It's the telecoms people! They've been laying new undersea cable for weeks now. It'll be them.

MAGS   Are you sure?

PETER   Yes. I was talking to a bloke the other day. He works at the harbour masters office. He said they were going to have a ship and mini-sub off the coast for at least six weeks. Anyway, turn it off. We can't listen to that beeping all day. It will drive us crackers. At least we know the sonar works now.

MAGS   Aye, aye, sir. Switching off sonar now. *(She flicks a switch and the beeping stops and the orange light disappears.)* Ooh, that was a real trip down memory lane! Do you remember when it was all beeping away down here and we used to make daily reports to the Admiralty?

JOAN   Yes. *(Sighing)* Happy days. Anyway *(Getting efficient)...* Pete...you've got to do the pigeons...I've got to do the cleaning...Mags has got to get lunch ready...and, Harry, you can come with me and sort out this backed-up toilet for us.

HARRY   *(enthusiastically grabbing his toolbox)* Lead the way, Joanie. I'm a dab hand at the old plumbing.

(MAGS and PETER exit, followed by JOAN, who takes the tea tray and HARRY.)

JOAN   *(pausing at the door)* Turn the lights off, Harry. We don't want to waste electricity, as we are paying for it and not the Navy.

HARRY   Righto. *(HARRY turns off the lights and closes the door behind them. The red light is still flashing. Then we hear a phone ringing in the darkness. Voices Offstage.)*

VOICE 1   Commodore Shelton's office.

VOICE 2   This is the Coastal Communications Department. We've had an unexplained signal from a disused Sea Reconnaissance Depot. We need the Commodore's call on this one.

VOICE 1   I'll put you through.

             (Pause)

VOICE 3   Shelton.

VOICE 2   Sorry to disturb you, ma'am, but we've had a signal from a disused Sea Reconnaissance Depot. Should we investigate?

VOICE 3   Good God! How long is it since the place was operational?

VOICE 2   About twenty years, ma'am.

VOICE 3   It's probably kids…breaking in and mucking about. Do we have anyone in the area who can go and check?

VOICE 2   Just a moment, ma'am, I'll ask Ops.

             (Pause)

             There's only a detachment of recruits doing training nearby.

VOICE 3   Are they armed?

VOICE 2   Yes, ma'am.

VOICE 3   Well send them over – but tell them for God's sake not to shoot anyone. We don't want the Navy dragged through the press for shooting a bunch of teenage vandals.

VOICE 2   Yes, ma'am. Will do.

             (Red Light goes out.)

BLACKOUT.

END OF SCENE 1.

BUNKERED
ACT I
SCENE 2

The same room, after lunch. Still in the dark. The red light has stopped flashing. The door opens and MAGS is in the shaft of light from the doorway. She turns the light on and goes to get her sewing things out again. HARRY enters, with his toolbox.

HARRY	That was the best cottage pie I've tasted in a long time, Mags.
MAGS	Thank you Harry. I wanted to be a cook in the Navy, when I joined up. I had all the City and Guilds certificates, as well. But, typical of the Services, they put me in Communications instead.
HARRY	*(going over to the machinery)* Yeah, that is typical of the Armed Services. They don't care about your talents – they just want cannon-fodder.
MAGS	I don't think Communications is what you'd call "cannon-fodder". At the time, it's only the sort of job women were allowed to do. Naval Support personnel. On land. You know.
HARRY	Yeah, well I sort of agree with that. I don't think women should be sent to the front line – whether it's a ship or in a tank. Not right.
MAGS	*(surprised)* Well, I wouldn't have thought you would have those outmoded ideas, Harry! I thought that "come the revolution", men, women and children were supposed to man the barricades.

HARRY	*(patiently explaining)* Mags, you are confusing me with a Communist. Anarchy is about the overthrow of established order.
MAGS	Well isn't that what the Communists did?
HARRY	*(confused himself)* Well…yes…I suppose so. But what I mean is, I'm not a militant anarchist, I'm an individualist anarchist and I support anarcho-pacifism.
MAGS	Get away. I didn't know that there were different types of anarchists.
HARRY	Oh yes. There are those who want to overthrow the state by violent revolution and there are those, like myself, who support only self-defence and the non-violent overthrow of the state from within.
MAGS	Sorry, you've lost me. What does that mean?
HARRY	Well, people like me believe in changing the State machinery by infiltrating it and changing the structure and laws of that State. Doing it legally, if you like. Making society fairer by …well, keeping on top of the bad things that go on and trying to do something about it.
MAGS	So how do you, personally, do that, then?
HARRY	Well, I don't vote, for a start.
MAGS	How does that help society?
HARRY	Because I, and my brothers and sisters in the anarcho-pacifist movement, don't perpetuate the corruption and incompetence of Government by voting the same buggers in all the time.
MAGS	Oh.

(JOAN enters, carrying a mug of coffee.)

JOAN   *(suspicious)* What's he been saying?

MAGS   He's been explaining to me the anarcho-pacifist policies.

JOAN   Has he now? And what do you conclude from his explanation?

MAGS   That he doesn't vote.

JOAN   *(sarcastically to HARRY)* That's it, is it? That's all modern day anarchists do? Refrain from voting?

HARRY   *(irritated)* No! That's not all we do! There are other things...

JOAN   Like what?

HARRY   *(blustering)* We...we lobby the Government over human rights issues...we...er...gather intelligence about corporate and Government corruption...

JOAN   *(laughing)* Gather intelligence! What you and Daft Mick from down the road?

HARRY   Don't call him that.

JOAN   I don't call him that! Everyone else calls him that. He is daft, anyway. He's been a few anarchists short of a plot ever since he tried to blow up a postbox in 2004 and he burst an eardrum.

MAGS   What did he blow up a postbox for?

HARRY   He was protesting about the introduction of postal voting for the European Parliament elections.

MAGS   Why?

HARRY   Because it was an exercise in corruption! God knows how many of those postal votes were destroyed, forged or just ignored. Like everything else in Brussels, they don't account to anybody...do as they please...pay themselves what they like and bugger the rest of us.

MAGS   *(to JOAN)* He's got a point there, you've got to admit it.

JOAN   *(grudgingly agreeing)* Mmm.

HARRY   Anyway, I can't sit here talking politics all day. I've got more stuff to fix.

(HARRY turns his attention to the machines. PETER enters.)

PETER   I've just checked on the pigeons again. They're fine. I won't give them a training run today though. Not if Bill's in bed.

MAGS   Ooh, no! Much as he loves those pigeons, he won't thank you if he has to get out of bed to take them in. He's dying, you know.

PETER   *(alarmed)* Eh?

MAGS   So he says. *(Dramatically)* He's got the flu and he's dying!

JOAN   Is he bad then?

MAGS   *(firmly)* He's got a stinking cold, Joanie, that's all. But you know what men are like. Now, look, have you washed your hands, Peter?

PETER   Of course I have!

MAGS   Good, because I've got a little favour to ask you.

PETER   What's that then?

MAGS   I need you to put this wedding dress on...

PETER   What?

MAGS   Oh come on, love. You're exactly the same height as our

	Carol and I can't pin the hem up unless you put the dress on. Please?
JOAN	*(laughing)* Go on, Pete! We won't laugh, honest!
MAGS	Please, Pete?
JOAN	She'll only keep on.
PETER	Oh, alright then. The things I have to do for you women!
HARRY	'Allo, 'allo…that sounds interesting! Just what is it that you do for these women?
JOAN	Oh don't get excited! It's nothing like that!
PETER	No, mate, it's nothing like that. Over the years I've had to hold more skeins of wool out *(He demonstrates with his hands)* than you've had hot dinners…I've given foot rubs… painted toenails…
MAGS	Only 'cos I can't bend over like I used to…
PETER	…taken my pliers to broken zips that wouldn't undo…
HARRY	…aye,aye…it's getting more interesting…
PETER	…pinned up hems…
JOAN	…Oh and there was that time I brought the dog in and you did her anal glands for me…
	(Everyone makes a noise of disgust.)
HARRY	I think that's all a bit above and beyond, mate. Above and beyond.
PETER	You're telling me. But, this is a new one…trying on a wedding dress. Can I just put it on over my clothes?
MAGS	Of course, love. Just take your jacket off.
HARRY	Er…before you do that…can we have the power off again

for a few minutes? I just need to do this machine. What is this machine, by the way?

JOAN   That, my dear brother, is a thirty year old computer. One of the first to be set up in the early eighties.

HARRY   Blimey? Can you do much on it?

PETER   *(taking off his jacket)* No. It was used more like a word processor really. It just used to generate reports. But, before it packed up, we used to play Pong on it, didn't we girls?

MAGS   *(strapping a pincushion on her wrist)* Oh I wasn't sorry to see that pack up! You and Bill used to spend hours on the bloody thing. Beep! Beep! It was worse than the sonar. It used to do something else as well...and I should know, because I was in charge of it...but for the life of me, I can't remember.

HARRY   God, it's amazing to think how far and how fast the computer has developed since 1981 isn't it? I used to have one of those Amstrads.

JOAN   Yes, I remember you spending hours on the damn thing, doing the minutes of the Anarchists Against A Police State meetings. Whatever happened to that group?

HARRY   It disbanded in 1985 after the miner's strike. The Chairman joined the police force.

JOAN   Huh! *(She switches on all the storm lamps.)* That just about sums up the pillocks that you associate with – the chairman of an anti-police movement ends up joining the police force. I expect he got fast tracked because he put on his CV that he was the Chairman of the Anarchists Against a Police State Movement. Where is he now?

HARRY	Chief Constable of Glamorgan or something.
JOAN	*(triumphant)* Told you! *(Businesslike)* Right. I will go and switch the power off, as Pete is getting dressed for his wedding.
	(JOAN exits with one of the storm lamps whilst PETER is carefully helped into the wedding dress by MAGS.)
MAGS	You'll have to stand on a chair, Pete.
	(PETER obliges by standing on a chair. He looks a complete idiot. HARRY takes a picture of him with his mobile phone.)
PETER	*(annoyed)* Oy! What did you do that for?
HARRY	You look priceless mate. Absolutely priceless.
PETER	That picture better not end up on the internet, Harry, or I really will kill you.
	(The lights go out. The stage is lit by the storm lamps. HARRY starts to work on the computer. JOAN re-enters from the hall and does a double-take at the sight of PETER.)
JOAN	Oh my God! It's the Bride of Dracula! God, you gave me a turn!
PETER	*(disgruntled)* Ha, ha. Very funny.
MAGS	Now keep still, Peter, while I work my way, around this hem. *(She starts inserting pins around the bottom of the dress.)*
JOAN	Are you sure you can see, in this light? You don't want your Carol to have a wobbly hem do you?
MAGS	*(dryly)* I think that's the least of her worries, Joanie. Getting her up the aisle at all is going to be an achievement, never mind the dress.

JOAN	Why, is she having second thoughts?
MAGS	Oh no! She's all for getting married. It's just we're not too sure about her intended.
JOAN	Why is he a commitment-phobe? Not the marrying kind?
MAGS	Well... he seems keen enough. It's just that...let me put it this way...I think he might be happier wearing the frock than she is.
JOAN	*(aghast)* You mean...?
MAGS	*(nodding)* I fear it's the George Michael scenario all over again.
HARRY	Right. I think that's it! You can put the lights back on now.
JOAN	That was quick!
HARRY	Yeah. It was only the wires in the plug that had corroded. Nothing wrong with the innards of the beast.
	(JOAN exits with her storm lamp to put the lights back on.)
PETER	*(nervous of HARRY taking another picture)* Will you be much longer, Mags?
MAGS	Why? You got some urgent work to do?
PETER	I wish.
MAGS	I'll be ages yet. I've only done about a foot of the hem. Just be patient.
	(The lights come back on.)
	Oh that's better. I can see what I'm doing now.
	(JOAN re-enters and switches off the storm lamps.)
JOAN	Anyone fancy a cuppa?
HARRY	Please!

MAGS	Ooh yes!
PETER	Definitely.
MAGS	Er, no, Peter. Sorry. You are not spilling tea down this wedding dress. You'll just have to go without until I've finished. I'll make you a cup as soon as I've put the last pin in.
JOAN	Right. Three teas it is. *(She exits.)*
HARRY	This computer is booting up.
MAGS	*(leaving her sewing and going to the computer)* Let's have a look.
PETER	*(about to get down off the chair)* It could be something important.
MAGS	No! Don't move, Peter! You can see it from up there!
	(PETER sighs and stays where he is. They all look at the screen.)
HARRY	It's just a load of numbers.
MAGS	Mmm. It's repeating a load of numbers. Now, I've seen this before but I can't remember what it means. Oh! My memory is getting dreadful! It will probably tell us in the operations manual but I can't remember where I put that either!
PETER	*(helpfully)* Try the drawers underneath.
	(MAGS opens drawers but finds nothing.)
MAGS	No. There's nothing here. Oh God, whatever did I do with it?
PETER	Given that we never did much with that computer and, as I recall, we only ever had two emergency training exercises, I'm not surprised that you can't remember where you put the manual. Don't worry about it. Leave the computer switched on and I expect it will eventually tell us what it is

supposed to do. But, meanwhile, could you come back and get on with this dress? I feel a right burke up here and I may need a toilet break soon.

MAGS   Righto. *(She goes back to the hem.)*

HARRY   I have to say, Mags, despite the fact that an ugly looking bloke is wearing that dress, you've done a beautiful job on it.

PETER   Shut up!

MAGS   Thank you Harry. I love sewing, you know. In fact I wouldn't mind doing it for a living. A nice made-to-order wedding dress business would suit me down to the ground.

HARRY   Well, there you are then! That's what you should do with your time when your old man retires. Open up a shop.

(JOAN enters with the tray of tea and biscuits.)

MAGS   Mmm. You may be right, Harry.

JOAN   Good Lord! Did you just say my brother was right about something?

MAGS   *(laughing)* Don't worry, it was nothing political! Harry was just saying that I should open up a wedding dress shop when Bill retires.

JOAN   *(dismayed)* Oh! Leave me on my own down here, why don't you?

HARRY   Oh come off it, Joanie! You can't possibly want to spend the rest of your working life down in this bunker. For God's sake woman! There's a whole world out there. You could be doing stuff.

JOAN   *(thoughtfully sipping her cup of tea)* D'you know what, Harry? I actually love this place.

HARRY   Getaway.

JOAN   I do. I love being in the Navy and I love being down here in
            our own little world. I would miss it dreadfully if I had to
            give it up.

MAGS   She would. She was distraught when she thought we'd all
            been made redundant. That's why Pete and Bill went to the
            Admiralty to try and sort it out. Joan was so upset, she
            couldn't leave the house.

HARRY   What back in ninety one?

MAGS   Yes.

HARRY   Funny enough, I remember that. She said she had terrible flu
            and couldn't see anyone. Our mum was worried sick, on
            account of Joanie never, ever got ill.

JOAN   I remember you coming to the door and saying you
            wouldn't leave until you knew I was alright.

HARRY   Gawd, yes! And when you opened the window and shouted
            down at me, you looked so bad, I wondered if I should start
            arranging your funeral.

JOAN   Thank you dear.

HARRY   No but you did. Frightened the life out of me. But then, you
            suddenly got better. The next day you phoned everyone and
            said you were as right as rain.

MAGS   Oh that's 'cos we hatched our survival plan that night.

HARRY   Survival plan?

PETER   Yes...well...Bill and I came back from the Admiralty...this
            was the second time...and we'd been given the right
            runaround, I can tell you. When we came out of there, Bill
            looked at me and said "I don't think they are ever going to
            sort it out" and that was when we decided that we would all

carry on as normal.

JOAN   Well...we said that we would carry on as normal if our next
            lot of pay cheques came through...

MAGS   ...which they did.

JOAN   And we decided how we would organise the money and
            stuff, for our retirement fund.

HARRY   Yeah, this retirement fund...how does that work then?

JOAN   Well, we all decided that we would pay a certain amount
            each month to be paid into various interest-bearing
            accounts. Then, when Bill and Peter retired, we would split
            it up four ways and each of us could then re-deposit it,
            where we wanted, to get a bit of a pension...just in case the
            Navy decided that we weren't entitled.

HARRY   Ah, yes, but you should definitely get a pension though –
            based on the years that you had put in *before* you were
            supposed to have been made redundant. Plus you should
            have got a redundancy payout.

JOAN   That's true. But suppose they found out about their mistake
            and made us pay back all the salaries we've had for the last
            twenty years?

HARRY   Nah. They wouldn't do that. It's their mistake. They'd look
            pretty bloody stupid if you took them to an industrial
            tribunal, wouldn't they? The press would have a field day!
            There'd be questions in Parliament and everything!

PETER   (*excited*) That's right! I think you're on to something there,
            Harry!

HARRY   So how much have you got in this retirement fund, if you don't mind me asking?

PETER   No. I'm quite proud of the investments I've made. Hand me my jacket, mate, and I'll tell you.

(HARRY hands PETER his jacket. PETER fumbles about in the pocket and produces a small notebook, then he hands his jacket back to HARRY, who puts it back on the chair.)

PETER   *(opening the notebook and smiling)* As a matter of fact, I checked the balances last night, online, and we have the grand total of one hundred and forty seven thousand pounds and forty five pence.

(Everyone expresses delight and HARRY whistles appreciatively.)

MAGS   Well! You know, I just never thought about that money at all. I just handed over my contribution every month and never gave it another thought!

JOAN   You've done well, Peter. Good lad.

HARRY   I should say he has! You'll be able to open a chain of wedding dress shops now, Mags.

MAGS   Oh I think one would be quite enough!

HARRY   Joanie, I don't suppose I could have a fag, could I?

JOAN   You suppose right, Harry. If you want to indulge your filthy habit, you'll have to go outside the bunker.

HARRY   *(disappointed)* Oh. Righto. But how do I find my way to the front door – as I was blindfolded when I came here…

JOAN   *(interrupting)* Did you say blindfolded?

HARRY   Yes. Pete blindfolded me, so I wouldn't know where we were going.

JOAN   Harry...I know you are a bit mental but in what universe does a bloke allow another bloke to blindfold him and take him on a car ride? Peter could have been a serial killer for all you know.

HARRY   *(scornfully)* What, Peter? Talk sense!

MAGS   Ah, you never know. He could have been abducting people all his life and was running out of options.

JOAN   Don't they teach you anything in the Anarchists Society? Here's another option – for all you know, Peter could have been a government spook who had been trained to eliminate enemies of the state.

(They all look at PETER thoughtfully.)

HARRY   Nah. Not Pete.

PETER   *(sarcastically)* It's alright, just talk about me as though I'm not here.

HARRY   *(having second thoughts)* Although you really don't know, do you? I mean I thought I knew my own sister and then I discover she's had a secret life for the last thirty or more years.

JOAN   There you are then. It just goes to show that you never really know about people.

MAGS   Yeah. Like George Michael and Richard Chamberlain.

JOAN   *(disagreeing)* Oh, I think we all knew about them, Mags. It just that some women choose to delude themselves. I call it the Freddie Mercury Syndrome. How many women fantasised about Freddie Mercury for God's sake?

HARRY   Anyway. Instructions to get out and back into this place, please. I'm dying for a fag.

PETER	Go out of this door…turn right…walk to the end of the corridor…turn left and the main entrance door is in front of you. Got that?
HARRY	Turn right, walk to the end, turn left. Got it.
JOAN	And when you get to the entrance door, *(Handing him the keys from her belt.)* I shouldn't do this – but here's the keys. You have to use the big one to unlock the door from inside. Make sure you lock it firmly behind you, when you're outside and you have to deadlock it from the inside when you come back in. Got that?
HARRY	*(taking the keys and grumbling)* Gordon Bennett! The Cold War's over you know! Who's going to invade now?
JOAN	*(being firm)* I like to do everything by the book. If we left this place unlocked, even for a second, we could have squatters, tramps or travellers taking it over. Or it could be vandalised by kids. You can't be too careful.
	(HARRY exits and closes the door behind him.)
	So, Mags, are you seriously thinking about opening up a dress shop, then?
MAGS	Well, it's a thought. Your brother put the idea in my head and now it's buzzing around in there like an excited little bee. You could always come in with me, Joanie! Be a business partner. You're so good at organisation. You could do all the paperwork and stuff. What about it?
JOAN	What me? In a dress shop? Sorry Mags but it's not my scene, really. *(Hastily)* I mean I can see that it would suit you down to the ground – but me? The Navy's always been my life…you know that.

PETER	Well, you won't be able to stay down here on your own, Joanie. I mean, you're not getting any younger. Supposing you had a heart attack or something?
JOAN	Oh cheer us all up, why don't you? I could just as easily have a heart attack at home....where I live...*(Emphasising)* alone. Anyway, don't talk about it. You and Bill don't retire for another six months. We don't have to talk about it now.

(Suddenly, there is a knock at the door and everyone jumps.)

JOAN	Ooh! *(Shouting)* Harry! Stop playing silly buggers! You nearly frightened us all to death!
HARRY	*(voice from behind the door)* Er...Joan? Could you open the door, please? My hands are otherwise occupied.
JOAN	*(annoyed)* What's he playing at? I'll give him "otherwise occupied"!

(JOAN strides towards the door and flings it open, to reveal HARRY, kneeling, with his hands on his head, flanked by two Marines, in combat gear and helmets, pointing machine guns into the room.)

JOAN	*(screams)* Oh My God!

(BLACKOUT)

(In the darkness we hear a telephone ringing.)

VOICE 1	Commodore Shelton's office.
VOICE 2	It's Communications here, again. Would you tell the Commodore that we've had a radio report from the training platoon that they have entered the bunker.
VOICE 1	And?
VOICE 2	No news yet. I just thought she would like to know.

VOICE 1   Well I won't tell her until you've got some more news. She's
               in a meeting anyway. Ring me back when you have
               something else to tell me.

VOICE 2   Will do.

               (END OF SCENE 2.)

BUNKERED
ACT I
SCENE 3

Everyone is in exactly the same position as at the close of Scene 2.

MAGS   Dear God! They've sent the Marines!

JOAN   *(to the Marines)* Now this is not what it looks like…

CONNOR   *(stepping into the room)* What it looks like *(Eyeing up PETER)* is a transvestite warrant officer's dressmaking club.

PETER   *(annoyed)* Oy! Respect for elders!

JOAN   Harry! Get up!

CONNOR   *(to HARRY)* You! Stay where you are! *(To JOAN)* I'll be the one to tell people what to do. *(Motioning with his gun to the other side of the stage)* All of you – except the bloke in the frock – over there.

             (MAGS and JOAN look irritated but they both move over to the other side of the stage.)

JOAN   I suspect that I outrank you, sonny.

CONNOR   That could very well be true but, since I was told by HQ that this site was decommissioned, and therefore I suspect you are all a sad bunch of fantasists who like dressing up in naval uniform and play acting down here – plus I have a gun – I think that makes me the law around here, don't you?

JOAN   *(fuming)* We are not, as you call it, 'a sad bunch of fantasists', we are serving Royal Navy personnel. Mags! Show him your dogtags!

(MAGS fumbles in her pocket and produces a key ring with lots of keys on. She goes up to CONNOR and sticks it under his nose.)

MAGS   There!

CONNOR   That's a Tesco's ClubCard.

MAGS   *(irritated)* Further along the key fob, you idiot!

CONNOR   *(taking the bunch of keys and examining the metal discs)* Fine. That's a set of dogtags. You can pick them up on the internet for a few quid. What does that prove?

JOAN   Look. I'm going to move now. I'm going over to the table and I'm going to pick up the day book. *(She does so and puts the open book in front of CONNOR's face.)* It shows that I…Second Officer Morris…signed in this morning at 0900 hours and I have duly signed all the others in…except for Leading Seaman Bill Potter, who's off sick.

CONNOR   *(shrugs)* Another part of your fantasy. And what's a Second Officer, anyway? There's no such rank.

JOAN   *(sighing)* Look…it's complicated. I *was* a Second Officer in the Wrens but *now* I should be a Lieutanant. Only…oh! How do I explain all this?

PETER   We'll have to tell him the whole story, Joanie…it's no good.

MAGS   *(to CONNOR)* Look…son…sorry, I don't know your name…could you just let Harry up off his knees and can we all sit down and have a cup of tea and talk about this?

            (There is a pause whilst CONNOR considers. Then he nods.)

CONNOR   OK. But don't try any funny stuff. I 'm still armed remember.

HARRY   I've been on my knees so long, I can't get up!

CONNOR	Midshipman – help the old geezer up.
TAYLOR	*(shouting)* Aye, aye, sir!
MAGS	I'll go and make some tea.
	(TAYLOR helps HARRY up and he rubs his knees and totters over to a chair. MAGS exits to make the tea.)
JOAN	*(acidly)* And could you please refrain from the ageist comments? Otherwise I shall have to continually refer to you as a Bootneck. What is your name and rank, by the way?
CONNOR	Sub-Lieutenant Connor, Platoon Weapons Instructor, Commando Training Wing and this *(points at TAYLOR) is* Midshipman Taylor, one of the most useless recruits it has been my misfortune to try and train.
JOAN	Right. As you know, I am Second Officer Morris, he *(Pointing at PETER)* is Chief Petty Officer Burrows, and the lady who has gone to make the tea is Leading Wren Potter. We were…are…the Naval Intelligence Unit in charge of this facility.
CONNOR	*(shaking his head)* I think I need to sit down. I'm a Commando – I can't get my head round all this.
PETER	*(exasperated)* Could someone help me down please?
CONNOR	Midshipman Taylor!
TAYLOR	Aye, aye, sir!
CONNOR	Help the o…the bloke in the frock get down off the chair.
TAYLOR	*(shouting)* Aye, aye, sir!
JOAN	Does she have to shout like that?
CONNOR	Of course she does. That's what we do.

TAYLOR	*(putting down her gun and helping PETER off the chair)* That's a very nice dress...
PETER	*(beaming)* Thank you.
CONNOR	*(wearily)* Less of the comments, Taylor.
TAYLOR	*(quietly)* Aye, aye, sir!
PETER	I really do want to get this dress off.
JOAN	Well you'd better wait for Mags, otherwise she'll kill you if *you* split a seam or something.

(MAGS enters with a tray of tea, sugar and spoons.)

MAGS	Yes, I will kill you. Just let me sort the tea things out and I'll get the dress off you. Bring that table over to the centre, will you, Harry?

(HARRY gets up and obliges but when he sets the table down in the centre, one leg is shorter than the rest.)

HARRY	Blimey, that's no good! Pete! Give us that book that was holding up the table leg!

(PETER retrieves the manual and looks at it.)

PETER	Here, Mags...I've found your operations manual for the computer!
MAGS	Oh, for goodness sake! No wonder I couldn't find it in the drawers. Find something else to put under the table leg. I need to read that.

(PETER finds a telephone book and puts it under the table leg. MAGS puts down the tea things and takes the Operations Manual. PETER and HARRY gather the other chairs around the table and sit. CONNOR moves his chair to the table. JOAN and MAGS sit. TAYLOR stands. MAGS

starts to read the manual, inbetween contributing to the conversation.)

TAYLOR   Can I take my helmet off sir?

CONNOR   Yes.

TAYLOR   Thank God for that. It's made one ear go numb. *(She takes off her gloves, revealing bright nail varnish, and reaches for a mug of tea.)*

CONNOR   Midshipman! Is that nail varnish you're wearing?

TAYLOR   *(guiltily)* Yes sir.

CONNOR   I'm going to put you on a bloody report for that! How many times?!

TAYLOR   This will be my third report, sir.

CONNOR   *(exasperated)* In a week, Taylor! In a week! *(sighs in despair)* I hate this bloody job. *(decisive)* Right. You lot. Explanations, please.

PETER   It's quite simple. When the navy decided to decommission this bunker in 1991, they forgot about us.

CONNOR   What do you mean?

JOAN   *(sarcastically)* I know you're a Marine, dear, and therefore not gifted in the intellect department but what is it about the word 'forgot' that you don't understand?

            (TAYLOR sniggers.)

CONNOR   *(annoyed)* I understand the word 'forgot' – I just don't understand how the Navy could 'forget' four intelligence personnel.

HARRY   You and me both, mate.

CONNOR	Who are you?
HARRY	*(indicating JOAN)* Her brother.
JOAN	Who is, I may add, an unauthorised person down here.
HARRY	I'm just the handyman.
PETER	I brought him down here to mend some of the equipment.
CONNOR	Hang on a minute. Let's backtrack here. You said the Navy 'forgot' you...that still doesn't explain why you are actually here.
JOAN	They carried on paying us, so we carried on doing our jobs!
CONNOR	I might be stupid but why didn't you just pocket the money and stay at home?
HARRY	*(agreeing with him)* It's what any normal person would have done.
JOAN	*(affronted)* No, it's what a devious, cheating, backslider would do, Harry! We are all honourable members of Her Majesty's Royal Navy...
PETER	God bless her...
JOAN	*(giving PETER a funny look)* ...quite...and as such, we all decided to work for our pay...for as long as it lasted.
CONNOR	Well...I have to admire your loyalty. I'm not sure I would have done the same in your place.
PETER	That's because you are a different generation. Anybody under forty has absolutely no idea about honour and commitment.
CONNOR	Is that right? I think you've been down in this bunker too long mate. You want to try having day to day dealings with

the Ministry of Defence and then see how you feel about honour and commitment. We don't have enough bloody equipment when we go into action and when we come home they threaten us with mass redundancies. You try feeling honourable about that!

JOAN   True. Life in the Services is not what it was.

PETER   So, why are *you* here? Has the Navy finally rumbled us?

HARRY   It's a bit heavy-handed, sending in a platoon of Marines isn't it? I nearly died of a heart attack when I opened the door.

JOAN   How many of them are out there, then?

CONNOR   Fifty two.

MAGS   Fifty two Marines! All armed?

CONNOR   Well, they've all got guns, but only I've got ammunition. They're in training. You don't think I'd leave over fifty wet-behind-the ears teenagers alone with armed weapons do you?

PETER   But I repeat my question…why are you here?

CONNOR   Because you sent a distress signal.

EVERYONE   What!?!

JOAN   We never did!

CONNOR   All I know is that HQ received a distress signal – enemy sighting, they said, and they figured, as we were the closest, we should come and investigate. I was expecting to find kids messing about down here, having vandalised some equipment or something. Instead I find a load of senior citizens in a time warp.

JOAN   This is all your fault, Peter! If you hadn't got Harry to repair the equipment, we wouldn't have, accidentally, sent off a signal.

MAGS   It says in the manual that, if an enemy sighting is made on the R591 machine – that's the one over there that Harry got working first – and it is not countermanded – which we didn't do, 'cos we forgot we were supposed to do it – a red light – over there *(She points)* – will start flashing to indicate that Naval HQ have been informed of the incident.

PETER   Well, I didn't see a red light flashing, did you?

JOAN   No.

HARRY   Not me.

MAGS   *(carrying on reading)* Ah, well that would be because the red light should then go out as a signal to *us* that Naval HQ have received and understood.

HARRY   You've got to hand it to the Navy. They've obviously kept all their systems up to scratch.

JOAN   *(worried)* I vaguely remember the procedure now and I'm sure that there is something else that we're supposed to do…

MAGS   Hang on a minute… *(She leafs through the manual.)* it's referring me to page four hundred and three. God, who writes these bloody manuals? They're so complicated!

HARRY   You'll probably find that it's a translation from Japanese.

PETER   What?

HARRY   Well, half the equipment's Japanese! The Navy probably bought a job lot off the Japanese Navy and got someone to translate the manuals.

CONNOR   That wouldn't surprise me.

MAGS   Ah! Now, it has something to do with that computer that
            Harry recently switched on. The one that's churning out all
            the numbers. It says....*(There is a pause while she quickly
            scans the page.)* Oh God!

JOAN   *(anxious)* What!?

MAGS   We should have stopped the computer, otherwise it sends a
            signal to HQ to say that we have been compromised and...

PETER   ...compromised? What does that mean?

MAGS   It means that we've been overrun by the Russians, you idiot!

JOAN   *(clapping her hands to her face in horror)* Oh no! I know
            what the next step is! It's...it's...

            *(Suddenly a klaxon starts blaring, the overhead lights start
            flashing and a robotic voice starts saying "LOCKDOWN",
            "LOCKDOWN", "LOCKDOWN". Everyone jumps up
            and scatters. JOAN tries to stop the computer, CONNOR
            and TAYLOR grab their guns and exit, MAGS hides her
            face in the manual, HARRY grabs his toolbox and exits to
            the power source, PETER, still in the wedding dress,
            generally flaps around. After a minute of mayhem, all sound
            stops and the lights go out. There is silence. After a pause, a
            flashing torch is seen in the doorway and HARRY
            reappears.)*

HARRY   I had to cut the wires to stop all the hoo-ha, so we're
            temporarily without lights. Sorry.

            *(PETER switches on a battery powered lamp and puts it on
            the table. JOAN fetches another one, switches it on and puts
            it on top of the computer. There is dim light all round.
            CONNOR and TAYLOR come running back into the room.)*

CONNOR	The front door can't be opened! We're trapped.
TAYLOR	*(enthusiastically)* It's exciting, isn't it?
CONNOR	*(losing it)* No! It is not exciting! It's terrible! I HAVE TO GET OUT OF HERE! *(He rushes out again.)*
JOAN	What's got into him?
	(In the distance we can hear CONNOR kicking and banging on the metal door and screaming "Is anybody there?" "Can you hear me?" This carries on throughout the following:)
	Harry, I think you'd better take your torch and bring Sub-Lieutenant Connor back here. He obviously needs to calm down.
HARRY	Why me? He's a big tough Marine – he might do me a mischief.
TAYLOR	*(enthusiastically)* I'll go. I'm trained for this sort of thing. If he gets violent, I'll just knock him out. I got top marks on the Attack by Stealth course. But *(To HARRY)* you'd better come with me because I shall need your help to drag his body back in here.
JOAN	Oh my God! You're not going to kill him are you?
TAYLOR	No, don't be daft. Come on.
	(TAYLOR runs off, followed by a reluctant HARRY. The noise offstage is reduced to murmurs as TAYLOR negotiates with CONNOR.)
MAGS	*(surfacing from the manual)* This is all *my* fault...
JOAN	Don't be silly. It's not your fault. It's Peter's fault.
PETER	Why is it *my* fault?

JOAN	Because if you had left the equipment alone to quietly rot away, we wouldn't have this problem, would we?
PETER	No, I suppose not. I was only being conscientious.
JOAN	Hmm. That didn't work though, did it? Leave well enough alone, that's my motto. *(CONNOR suddenly starts shouting " I've got to get out!" followed by a quick "Aargh!". Then silence.)* What is going on out there?
	(TAYLOR and HARRY appear, dragging CONNOR's unconscious body between them. The torch is balanced on CONNOR's stomach. They lay him in the middle of the room. TAYLOR looks pleased with herself.)
JOAN	Is he alright?
TAYLOR	He'll have a bit of a headache when he wakes up, that's all. He was becoming hysterical. I had to do it.
HARRY	*(admiring)* I've never seen anything like it. She did this sort of Vulcan Death Grip on his neck and he was spark out!
PETER	*(puzzled)* Vulcan Death Grip?
HARRY	Star Trek, mate. The Vulcans…they do this sort of thing on the side of the neck that knocks people out *(He demonstrates but PETER just shakes his head.)*…oh never mind.
MAGS	*(amazed)* They didn't teach us that in the Wrens. And it would have been so useful on Saturday nights.
JOAN	Well that's all very well, but what do we do when he comes round?
PETER	Take his gun away, for a start.
HARRY	Good thinking, Bride of Dracula. *(He takes CONNOR's*

	gun from TAYLOR, who had it slung over her shoulder.) I'll go and lock this in the store cupboard. *(HARRY exits.)*
PETER	Mags, will you please take this dress off me!?
MAGS	*(rushing over to him)* Oh of course, love, I'm sorry.
	(MAGS and JOAN begin to carefully lift the dress over PETER's head and put it back on the dress form.)
TAYLOR	Well. What happens now?
JOAN	I have absolutely no idea, as we have never been through this scenario.
PETER	The computer still seems to be working.
	(They all crowd round it and their faces are bathed in a blue light.)
JOAN	What does it say in the manual?
	(MAGS goes back to the table and starts leafing through the manual by lamp light.)
MAGS	Um…let me see…ah! Apparently, we have to wait until HQ send a detachment with the code and open the door from the outside, using the keypad.
JOAN	Well that doesn't fill me with hope. First of all, we don't know if the system completely works and that HQ will have got the signal that we are locked down. Secondly, we don't know if they will be able to find the code in the archives anywhere and, thirdly, we don't know if the keypad still works or whether it has rusted to hell.
PETER	*(slumping down in a chair)* Well, that's it then. We're sealed in here for eternity. We'll all die down here and no-one will ever know.

MAGS	Oh, get a grip, Pete!
TAYLOR	You're forgetting that there are fifty one trainee Marines outside the door. They're bound to raise the alarm when it gets dark and we still haven't come out. *(She gets out her mobile phone.)* Do these work down here?
MAGS	No.
TAYLOR	Oh that's a pity. I've got an Emergency Situation App and I've been dying to use it.
JOAN	Still, if the worst comes to the worst, the marines could always get the fire brigade to cut us out, couldn't they?
PETER	Talk sense, woman. That's a six inch steel door which was constructed to keep enemy invaders out. It's going to take a lot more than the fire brigade to get through that lot.
TAYLOR	*(brightly)* I also got top marks on my explosives course! We could construct a bomb!
JOAN	With what?
TAYLOR	You'd be surprised. I'll go and have a look in your store room and kitchen. *(TAYLOR exits, meeting HARRY returning. To HARRY)* This is such fun!
HARRY	Where's she going?
PETER	To make a bomb.
HARRY	Blimey! I bet she doesn't have many boyfriends – what with the Vulcan Death Grip and the bomb making expertise, she'd be a right no no.
JOAN	*(slumping down in another chair)* This isn't how I pictured my career ending.
PETER	Bang goes my pension.

HARRY   Don't say 'bang' Pete...under the circumstances.

MAGS   I don't suppose I'll make the wedding now. Whatever is our
             Carol going to do, without a wedding dress?

MUSIC, LIGHTS *Storm lamps go out simultaneously.*

END OF ACT I.

INTERVAL.

BUNKERED
ACT II

MUSIC. The LIGHTS stay black. MUSIC fades. In the darkness we hear a telephone ringing. Voices Offstage.

VOICE 1	Commodore Shelton's office.
VOICE 2	Coastal Communications here. There's been even more trouble at that disused Sea Reconnaissance depot. I need to speak to the Commodore.
VOICE 1	Hang on I'll put you through.
SHELTON	Shelton.
VOICE 1	Sorry to disturb you, ma'am, but we've had a signal from the Disused Sea Recon bunker and it's gone into lockdown. Plus we've had a signal from the platoon of trainee marines that they are all standing outside of the place and their platoon commander and one of the recruits are trapped inside.
SHELTON	Jesus! What the hell is going on down there? Right. I'd better go myself. Do we have access codes for the facility?
VOICE 1	We're looking them out now, ma'am. But we're having to scour the archives for them, as it's been defunct for twenty years.
SHELTON	Well, when you find them, give them to my driver and then send him round to pick me up. And I want a complete information blackout on this – understand?

VOICE 1	Yes, ma'am.
SHELTON	The last thing we want is the press getting hold of this piece of, what I can only assume, is spectacular incompetence.
VOICE 1	Yes, ma'am.

(There is the sound of a phone being put down.)

(All the storm lamps come on simultaneously, to reveal everyone in the same position, except for CONNOR, who is now sitting with his head in his hands, quietly groaning.)

CONNOR	Oh my head.
JOAN	You were hysterical. Your midshipman had to knock you out.
CONNOR	I know. I remember.
PETER	Are you alright now, son?
CONNOR	Apart from a splitting headache, I suppose so.
MAGS	Whatever made you get in such a state?
CONNOR	Claustrophobia. I had to come out of the Submarine Service because of it. It was when I realised that we were locked in…I just panicked. I suppose we are still locked in?
JOAN	I'm afraid so. Are you likely to panic again?
CONNOR	I can't guarantee I won't.
JOAN	In that case *(She goes and gets her handbag and produces a bottle of pills)*… I think you should have one of these.
CONNOR	*(eyeing it suspiciously)* What is it?
JOAN	A sedative.
CONNOR	No. I can't do that. I have to be in command of the situation.

JOAN	I'm afraid – as senior officer – I must insist. I feel that you are a risk to the personnel and, unless you take this pill, we will have to restrain you.
CONNOR	What?!
PETER	She's right. We'll have to tie you up.
CONNOR	I'd like to see you try.
HARRY	Well, maybe they might have a problem, but I don't think Superwoman out in the kitchen will.
CONNOR	Where is Midshipman Taylor?
MAGS	Making a bomb.
CONNOR	What!!! *(He tries to stagger to his feet but then has to collapse on a chair because he is still dizzy.)*
JOAN	Don't worry. I don't imagine she'll be very successful. Not unless she can make a bomb out of rich tea biscuits and washing up liquid...cos that's all we've got in the kitchen. Take the sedative, Sub Lieutenant Connor – that's an order. *(CONNOR reluctantly takes the pill and washes it down with some tea offered by PETER.)*
MAGS	*(taking JOAN to one side)* Whatever do you carry sedatives for?
JOAN	*(confidentially)* I don't. They're the cat's worming pills, I picked them up this morning. It might give him the runs a bit later but that's all. The point is, he *thinks* it's a sedative, and that might just calm him down for a bit.
MAGS	*(sniggering)* Unless he coughs up a fur ball and gets wise.
JOAN	*(smiling)* Sshh. *(Turning back to CONNOR)* So, we're hoping that your marines are well–enough trained to raise

	the alarm and get us all out of here.
CONNOR	*(gloomily)* I wish I could say they were but they are the most useless shower I've ever dealt with.
PETER	Oh dear. That's not good is it? What's wrong with them?
CONNOR	Too spoilt. They can't cope with getting up early; going to bed early; living without their X boxes and play stations; doing basic training…all of it. Totally useless. We lost ten of them in week nine after the gym pass out…
JOAN	Didn't like it?
CONNOR	No. They passed out – literally. Then three of them sunk during the battle swim test…
PETER	Oh, yeah…but that one is hard…I remember when I tried out for the Marines…
JOAN	*(disbelief)* The Marines? You?
PETER	*(defensively)* I was young and fit, once!
MAGS	But not fit enough for the Marines – obviously.
PETER	*(annoyed)* Well, I'd like to see you try and swim in open sea with a thirty two pound pack on your back!
MAGS	Huh! That's nothing! Most women have to get in a supermarket shop whilst balancing a squirming thirty two pound toddler on their hip! I'd like to see the Marines try that one!
JOAN	I've often thought that women have more stamina than men.
CONNOR	Actually, they do. Men are stronger in quick bursts but the women that have come through basic training do seem to have staying power.
PETER	*(uncomfortable)* Yes…but you can't have a Marine corps

made up entirely of women, can you? We'd be the laughing stock of the world.

HARRY   I dunno. I bet having an all female Marine corps wouldn't bother the Israelis. And, I bet if they were all like La Femme Nikita out in the kitchen, the enemy wouldn't stand a chance.

CONNOR   I'd better go and stop her blowing herself up. *(He stands up and sways a little.)* I tell you what…that sedative packs a powerful punch! I can feel it working all ready. *(CONNOR exits.)*

MAGS   *(laughing)* And off he goes – to do a bit of tom catting!

PETER   *(suspicious)* What's she laughing at?

JOAN   I gave the Marine one of my cat's worming tablets.

HARRY   Ingenious. I've always said that about you, Joanie. You always come up with solutions when there's a crisis.

JOAN   Thank you Harry. I suppose you all realise that we are well and truly scuppered now? The Navy knows we are here, which is why they sent the Marines in…and now that we've managed to lock ourselves in and we're going to have to be blown out of here by the commandos…well, it's all up for us, isn't it?

PETER   I know. They're going to court martial us. It would have been bad enough before – but now they're going to do us for damaging Government property.

MAGS   Not necessarily. We have completely forgotten our protocol.

JOAN   What do you mean?

MAGS   The blessed pigeons!

JOAN	Oh my God! Yes! If we send a pigeon and get Bill out of his sick bed, he can come down here and let us all out…
PETER	*(excited)* Then no-one will have to blow up the door!
HARRY	Or cut it, or whatever.
MAGS	Right. Bill will never forgive me for this, but it can't be helped.
JOAN	We'll have to write a note for the pigeon's leg.
PETER	And I'll go up and put it on. Which one shall I send?
MAGS	Doris. She's a noisy beggar. She coo-coo-cachoos fit to bust when she lands on our conservatory. And you never know whether Bill's been knocking back the Night Nurse.
HARRY	Pardon?
MAGS	You know – that cold medication. It fair knocks you out and we need to wake him up. Doris will do it.
JOAN	Right. I'll do the note. *(JOAN grabs a pad and a pen and starts to write, reading it out aloud as she does so.)*
	"BILL, we are trapped in the bunker. Come and get us out as quick as you can. The access code is …" Mags? What's the code?
MAGS	*(looking in the manual and reading out loud)* Oscar Tango Lima Four Five Two.
JOAN	*(writing)* O…T…L…four five two. Good. *(She gives the small strip to PETER.)* Right. Off you go Pete. Give Doris a kiss from us and tell her to go home.
PETER	Righto. *(PETER exits.)*
HARRY	This is all incredibly exciting!

JOAN	Mmm. For you. For me, it's incredibly depressing because I am finally going to have to give up being in the Navy.

JOAN   Mmm. For you. For me, it's incredibly depressing because I am finally going to have to give up being in the Navy.

MAGS   *(trying to be hopeful)* Well, you don't know, Joanie. They might let us stay on and see out our time – you never know.

JOAN   Thank you for trying to be positive, Mags, but I think we both know that's not going to happen.

HARRY   But, it's like I said before…they won't want the world to know that they left you down here and paid you for twenty years. Trust me. Plus, when you add in a few more details, like the Marine went berserk and you gave him a worming tablet, I reckon the report on this lot will go into the National Archives for seventy years, on the grounds that they will all look like complete idiots if it ever got out.

MAGS   He's right.

JOAN   That's twice you've been right today. I think I may have to go and lay down in a darkened room to recover.

HARRY   Ha, ha.

          (PETER comes rushing back in with a bloody handkerchief wound around his hand.)

PETER   *(panicking)* You'll have to pick another bird!

JOAN   Peter! Your hand! What's happened?

PETER   Doris has laid a clutch of eggs and she won't leave them. She gave me a right pecking when I tried to pick her up.

MAGS   Good grief! Didn't you notice she was broody when you fed them this morning?

PETER   *(looking dumbfounded)* What am I – a pigeon midwife? I wouldn't know a broody pigeon if it fell out of the sky on me! She was alright this morning. She obviously popped them out later.

JOAN   I bet it was the klaxon going off that sent her into early labour.

MAGS   Let's get that hand looked at. You don't want to get some horrible disease. The first aid box is in the kitchen, come on, Pete.

(MAGS and PETER exit to the kitchen.)

HARRY   *(putting his arm around JOAN)* Never mind, sis. Look at it this way...you could have a proper life now. I mean look at you...never married...stuck down in a concrete bunker all your life. God! You're like one of those Russian dissidents whose been stuck in a gulag for thirty years. You're going to need some serious counselling to get beyond this you know.

JOAN   Don't talk daft, Harry. I only work here from nine to five. I go shopping, belong to the WI and volunteer at the local hospital. I haven't been in Siberia for the last thirty years. I'm more likely to need counselling after shopping in Tesco's on a Saturday than I am working in a Cold War bunker. At least there's no screaming kids down here.

HARRY   True. You see, Joanie. You and I are not so different. We're both natural loners, obsessed with the organisation of the realpolitik of life.

JOAN   Except that I am sane and you are bonkers.

HARRY   *(taking his arm away in a huff)* Please yourself. I was just trying to reach out to a lost soul, that's all.

JOAN   *(trying to apologise)* Look...sorry...Harry. I'm just a bit pre-occupied at the moment. I appreciate the gesture. OK?

(PETER and MAGS come back with TAYLOR. PETER's hand is nicely bandaged. In the distance can be heard a faint tapping of metal on metal.)

MAGS

There we are...he's all disinfected and bandaged and ready to have another go. This time he's going to try Arthur. He doesn't coo as much as Doris but the evil little beggar scratches away at our conservatory roof like nobody's business. Either the scratching will wake Bill up or the smashing of glass as Arthur finally scratches up all the putty that holds it in place. I'm trying to be cheerful but, deep down, I'm fearing for my conservatory.

JOAN

What is that tapping noise?

TAYLOR

It's the chief trying to signal to my classmates in morse code on the door.

HARRY

Will that work?

PETER

Nah. That door's six inches thick.

TAYLOR

Plus the fact that no-one in the platoon...and I mean no-one...passed their morse code test last week. Actually, I think he's beginning to panic again.

HARRY

The cat wormer didn't work then?

TAYLOR

Sorry?

JOAN

Shut up, Harry. How did the bomb-making go?

TAYLOR

(shaking her head) Not good. I couldn't find the right ingredients.

JOAN

Well, that's a bit of a relief, in a way. Go and fetch your man. I think a bit of diversion is in order.

TAYLOR

Righto.

(TAYLOR exits. PETER goes to the table and retrieves TAYLOR's combat gloves and puts them on.)

PETER   Right. Operation carrier pigeon. Mark two.

JOAN   That's a good idea. The gloves.

PETER   Well, I've got to get past Doris to get to Arthur. I'm not getting pecked to death again. *(PETER exits.)*

MAGS   I think he's very upset.

HARRY   What, about the pecking?

MAGS   No. He feels it's all his fault that we're in this mess.

JOAN   Well it is. I've got no sympathy. If he wasn't such an old fusspot we could have carried on here indefinitely. *(Changing tack.)* Where's the Scrabble board?

MAGS   In the drawer over there. Under the sonar.

JOAN   *(fetching the board)* It's time to sit down and have a relaxing game of Scrabble. That'll take his mind off his claustrophobia.

MAGS   Oh that's a good idea!

(JOAN lays out the Scrabble on the table and MAGS puts the chairs around, ready for a game. TAYLOR appears, leading CONNOR, who is twitching slightly.)

JOAN   Oh there you are! We're going to play a nice game of Scrabble while we wait for the help to arrive.

CONNOR   *(with an air of desperation)* What help? No-one's coming. We're trapped down here. All the recruits have sloped off back to barracks.

MAGS   Ah, but Peter's gone to send a carrier pigeon.

CONNOR   *(looking at her with horror)* This is how it starts, isn't it?
            Slowly, one by one, we all go mad. First it's mythical
            pigeons, then we'll all be hallucinating about our loved
            ones...

JOAN   Pull yourself together, Connor! The pigeons aren't mythical!
            We've got a roof full of highly trained Royal Navy carrier
            pigeons!

HARRY   *(reassuringly)* Straight up, mate. The pigeons are real.
            Honest.

CONNOR   *(giving a wobbly smile)* Really! So we might get rescued?

MAGS   Of course we will. My Bill will rouse himself from his sick
            bed and he'll be round as quick as a flash. You'll see.

JOAN   In the meantime, we're going to play a nice game of
            Scrabble to calm us all down. You sit down there, Connor.
            I'll go and make us a nice cup of tea.

TAYLOR   I'll help you.

JOAN   Good girl.

            (TAYLOR and JOAN exit.)

HARRY   *(helping a rather frail CONNOR into a chair and speaking
            to him like a child)* There we are. Everything's going to be
            fine. You see.

            (MAGS starts doling out the squares to everyone.)

MAGS   We can play five but I don't think we've got enough for six.

HARRY   Well, I don't mind being left out. I'll just help the Marine
            here. *(To CONNOR)* We'll do it together, eh?

            *(CONNOR nods gratefully and HARRY puts his chair next
            to him. PETER comes back, looking pleased with himself.)*

PETER	Well, that's all done, then.
HARRY	Old Arthur hadn't changed sex and popped out a few eggs then?
PETER	No. I think he was glad to be out of there. Doris is pecking every bird that comes with six inches of her precious eggs. All the rest of them are all huddled up in one corner of the roost looking fed up.
CONNOR	*(grasping HARRY's jumper anxiously)* They're talking about the pigeons aren't they?
HARRY	*(putting his arm around CONNOR's shoulder and reassuring him)* Yes, that's right. The real carrier pigeons… up in the loft.
	(PETER gives HARRY and CONNOR a funny look. MAGS taps his arm and makes a sign (finger circles to the head) that CONNOR is gaga. PETER sits down but moves his chair slightly away from CONNOR. JOAN and TAYLOR come back with the tea and start doling it out.)
JOAN	There we are – a nice hot, sweet tea for the Marine. *(She hands a mug to CONNOR.)* Now, we're going to play a nice game of Scrabble to take our minds off things. OK, Connor?
	(CONNOR nods but still occasionally twitches. JOAN sits down between PETER and CONNOR. TAYLOR draws up a computer chair between PETER and MAGS.)
PETER	You start, Joanie. Senior officer and all that.
JOAN	*(looking at her tiles)* OK. Let me see. Ah yes. *(She lays out seven letters on the board.)* T…R…A…P…P…E…D, trapped. *(CONNOR gives a small whimper but no-one*

notices.) That's one, two, three…nine…ten…twelve altogether. Who's keeping score?

MAGS I will. *(She turns over the manual, grabs a pencil and starts writing names in columns.)* That's twelve for Joanie. Your turn next Mr Connor.

HARRY *(still speaking to him as though he were a child)* OK mate. Let's have a look at what we've got…oh, yes…I think we can do this one. *(He rearranges the letters in front of CONNOR, who looks at him with a horrified expression but HARRY doesn't notice.)* Yep…there we go. *(He lays out the letters on the board.)* L…O…C…K…E…D, locked. That's one…two…five…ten…eleven…thirteen.

PETER Oh that was a good one. K's are good. Worth five points.

MAGS My turn now. Let's see. It needs to be a word that uses the top bit. Ooh,ooh! I think I've got it! *(She puts the letters on the board)* Right…B in front of Harry's O…then L…T…E… and D. bolted. *(CONNOR whimpers again.)* That's three for the B…four…five, six, seven, nine. Oh. Not as good as I thought it would be. Your turn Midshipman.

TAYLOR Righto. Actually, I've got one that uses up all my letters!

JOAN Ooh, you jammy devil! What is it?

TAYLOR *(laying out the letters on the board)* E…N…T…O…M…B, then a D on the other side of your E…that spells entombed…

(CONNOR cracks. He leaps to his feet and screams, then runs off out of the door. They all look at each other.)

PETER What set him off this time?

MAGS   Harry! Go and see where he's gone!

HARRY   *(grumbling but getting up)* Why is it always me? *(HARRY goes to the door and peeps round to the left.)* He's gone in the kitchen! *(Hurriedly)* He's coming out! *(He presses (himself flat against the back wall.)* He's got a knife!

              (CONNOR, screaming and clutching a butter knife goes running past the open door and on down the corridor. Then we hear him shouting at the front door and banging on it.)

PETER   He's gone back to the front door!

JOAN   Well, he's not going to do much damage with a butter knife.

MAGS   Not to the door…but he could hurt himself.

JOAN   Taylor! You'll have to do the grip thing again.

TAYLOR   *(sighing and getting up reluctantly)* Yes, ma'am. *(To HARRY)* You'll have to come with me again.

HARRY   *(to everyone)* Why is it always me?

              (TAYLOR and HARRY exit. JOAN starts to put away the Scrabble things. We hear some shouting in the corridor, then CONNOR goes "Aargh" and there is silence.)

JOAN   I don't feel like playing any more.

MAGS   No…me either.

JOAN   *(she hands the Scrabble box to PETER)* Put these away, Pete, would you?

              (PETER puts the Scrabble board away in the drawer under the sonar. MAGS and JOAN put the computer chair back and the other chairs against the wall. TAYLOR and HARRY return with CONNOR's body again and put him downstage, his feet towards the audience. The bent butter

knife is on CONNOR's stomach, which TAYLOR retrieves and holds up.)

TAYLOR   I'm afraid your butter knife's had it. He was trying to batter the door down with it.

JOAN   That man is going to have serious brain damage if you do that Vulcan Death Grip on him anymore.

PETER   We'll have to tie him up this time. We can't have him running amok again.

TAYLOR   I'll do it. I'm really good with ropes.

MAGS   Is there anything that you're not good at?

TAYLOR   Morse code...oh...and semaphore.

JOAN   *(indicating CONNOR)* I thought he said you were really useless.

TAYLOR   He did say to me...just before we came into the bunker... that I should come with him because I was the *least* useless in the platoon. He's alright. He's just an old style Marine and he has a hard time relating to women.

MAGS   God! You'd think in all the time we've been in the Service that things would have changed, wouldn't you?

JOAN   Fat chance. Although I do hear that there's a couple of female Commodores now.

             (TAYLOR gets some of HARRY's cut pieces of wire and starts to tie up CONNOR's legs.)

MAGS   Harry. Do you think you could restore the lights? I'd really like to press on with the hem on that dress, as we have nothing else to do.

HARRY   I'm on it. *(HARRY grabs his tool box and torch and exits.*

Suddenly we hear a clanging of a door and everyone reacts. In the corridor we hear HARRY shout.) (offstage) The cavalry's arrived! Hello, Bill, mate!

BILL   *(offstage)* Hello Harry, what are you doing here!

JOAN   Thank God, Bill's arrived!

MAGS   Ooh, I hope he's in a good mood!

(BILL appears in the doorway. He is wearing a coat over his pyjamas, and a scarf. As he appears, the main lights come on and he smiles and opens his arms.)

BILL   *(smiling)* Let there be light!

MAGS   How are you feeling, love?

BILL   Better. I was getting bored, if truth be told. Getting the message from Arthur perked me right up. Well, you lot got yourselves in a right pickle, didn't you?

PETER   Oh, it's been terrible! *(He switches off all the storm lamps).*

BILL   Did you get my message back?

MAGS   No! Did you send Arthur back then?

JOAN   We never thought to look!

BILL   *(scornfully, to MAGS)* No, I didn't send Arthur back! Think about your protocol, woman! Never send the same bird back, it just confuses them! No, I sent Sid.

MAGS   Oh my God! I forgot we had Sid at home.

PETER   Wait a minute! Isn't Sid the really old pigeon?

BILL   Yeah. I reckon he'd be about one hundred and two in human years. I had him at home because he needed a bit of peace and quiet but he got right excited when I decided to put a message on him and send him back. Bit of an outing for him, I reckon. I'll go and check on him.

(BILL takes his coat off and exits. HARRY re-appears.)

HARRY   I've just re-attached the lights. I daren't touch any of the other wiring in case that blessed klaxon and the robotic voice starts up again.

JOAN   Very sensible. Although, if memory serves me, once the keypad has received the access code, it should shut off the lockdown paraphernalia.

TAYLOR   *(straightening up)* Right. I've bound his feet. Now I'll start on his hands.

JOAN   I've got some paracetomol in my bag for when he wakes up. He's going to have a splitting headache again.

MAGS   I shouldn't be surprised if that worming tablet you gave him, sent him over the edge, you know.

TAYLOR   You gave him a worming tablet?

JOAN   Well...yes. But it was a cat's dose. A tiny little tablet. I persuaded him it was a sedative...you know...hoping that his mind would calm itself down if he thought he'd been sedated. Didn't work though, did it?

(BILL appears, holding a dead pigeon in his hands and looking distraught.)

BILL   Sid's dead!

MAGS   Oh no!

JOAN   Poor thing!

PETER   Sorry, mate. Was it too much for him?

BILL	No, it wasn't that. The poor beggar must have flown straight into the coop and on to Doris. She attacked him and he snuffed it. Doris has had eggs, by the way.
PETER	*(holding out his bandaged hand)* I know, mate. Believe me, I know.
BILL	*(mournfully)* Killed in the line of duty. Sid would have wanted it that way.
MAGS	We should bury him with honours.
JOAN	Eh?
BILL	No, she's right, Joanie. This bird has served Her Majesty's Government faithfully and deserves a proper funeral.
TAYLOR	*(helpfully)* I saw a box in the kitchen that would do as a coffin.
BILL	Thank you, dear.
	(TAYLOR exits.)
	I've just realised that she's a Marine. What's she doing here?
HARRY	We've got one spark-out on the floor, as well.
BILL	*(going over and taking a look)* Blimey! And he's tied up! What's all this about, then?
JOAN	I'm afraid the game's up for us, Bill. *(Taking a deep breath.)* Peter brought Harry in to bring the equipment up to scratch...
BILL	*(looking at PETER)* What?!
PETER	*(looking sheepish)* I know, I know. Big mistake.
JOAN	...so Harry, unwittingly, sets off a signal to Naval HQ. They send a troop of marines to investigate...meanwhile...

MAGS	...the computer started up and we couldn't find the manual...
BILL	*(shocked)* Mags!
JOAN	...so we went into lockdown.
PETER	The Marine on the floor was claustrophobic and went berserk...
JOAN	...several times, actually...
MAGS	...no, only twice...the second time was probably because Joanie gave him a cat's worming tablet...
BILL	...worming tablet?
MAGS	Yes...it's a long story...then he went bonkers again...
TAYLOR	*(re-appearing with a tin biscuit box)*...so I knocked him out and tied him up...well...I've still got his arms to do. Will this be suitable? *(She proffers the biscuit tin to BILL.)*
BILL	*(in a bit of a daze)* Yes, that will be lovely. *(He puts the dead pigeon in the box.)* So, that's it, then? The Navy have discovered us and the game is well and truly up?
JOAN	It looks like it. God knows who is on their way now...
	(SHELTON appears in the doorway.)
SHELTON	That would be me.
	(Everyone turns, sees SHELTON in full uniform and rapidly arranges themselves into two lines, come to attention and salute – except for HARRY, who is sitting in a chair near the body of CONNOR. SHELTON walks in between the two lines and returns salutes. She stops at CONNOR's body and looks.)
	At ease, everyone. *(Everyone moves to 'at ease', in the*

Naval position of arms folded behind the back and legs apart.) I see we have a casualty.

BILL   *(thinking she means the pigeon, holds up the box)* Yes, ma'am, killed in the line of duty, I'm afraid. I'm afraid Doris attacked him as he entered.

SHELTON   I see. And which one of you ladies is Doris?

JOAN   *(realising the error)* Oh no, ma'am! Doris is a pigeon. She killed Sid, who is also a pigeon.

SHELTON   *(still confused)* I see…I think. So who is this Marine on the floor?

PETER   Sub-Lieutenant Connor, ma'am. He's unconscious.

HARRY   Knocked out by a Vulcan Death Grip from Wonder Woman.

SHELTON   OK. Let me get this straight. A pigeon has been killed by another pigeon. Is that correct?

BILL   Yes, ma'am. Both Royal Naval Carrier pigeons on active duty.

SHELTON   Quite. And this Marine…Connor…was knocked out by?

EVERYONE   *(pointing at TAYLOR)* Her!

TAYLOR   *(coming to attention and saluting again)* Midshipman Taylor, ma'am!

SHELTON   *(going up to TAYLOR)* And why did you knock out your superior officer, Taylor?

TAYLOR   He was demented, ma'am!

SHELTON   Demented?

HARRY   Crazy. Went "postal". Loony, berserk…

SHELTON   *(interrupting)* Yes. Thank you. I get the picture. Now, would you all mind telling me exactly who you are and why you are here?

JOAN   *(coming to attention)* Second Officer Morris, ma'am. In charge of this facility.

PETER   *(coming to attention)* Chief Petty Officer Burrows, ma'am.

MAGS   *(coming to attention)* Leading Wren Potter, ma'am.

BILL   *(coming to attention)* Leading Seaman Potter, ma'am.

(SHELTON looks at HARRY, who grins, leaps to his feet and stands to attention.)

HARRY   Harry Morris, ma'am. Anarchist and general handyman!

SHELTON Right. Well that tells me who you all are but not what you are doing here.

JOAN   *(stepping forward one step and stamping her feet to attention)* As the senior officer, ma'am, I feel it is my duty to explain fully exactly what we are doing in this facility.

SHELTON Very well, Second Officer Morris. While you are explaining everything, which I have no doubt will be lengthy, perhaps you could also take me on a tour of the facility. It's been a long time since I was down in a Sea Recon bunker like this. I started my career in one just like it though, near Windscale.

JOAN   *(forgetting her rank)* Wait a minute...Windscale? Shelton? *(Breaking into a grin.)* You're little Marge Shelton! Don't you remember me? We were in basic training together! It's me...Joanie...remember? We climbed the wall many a time after dark...

SHELTON *(forgetting her rank and flinging her arms wide)* Joanie! I wondered what happened to you!

(SHELTON and JOAN hug and then cling on to each other, smiling.)

You were such a laugh! I learnt all my bad habits in the Wrens from you!

HARRY   Eh? This is my sister Joan, you're talking about!

SHELTON   Your sister was the naughtiest girl in the whole platoon!

JOAN   And look at you! A Commodore!

SHELTON   Yes. There's only five of us in the whole Navy. Women Commodores, I mean. It's been a struggle.

JOAN   Look, come to the kitchen and have a cuppa. I've got loads to tell you.

SHELTON   Lead the way, Joanie.

(SHELTON and JOAN exit, chatting away happily.)

PETER   Well, that was a turn up!

MAGS   Fancy them knowing each other.

BILL   Joanie might just be able to sweet talk the Commodore into saving our bacon.

PETER   Let's hope.

BILL   Meanwhile, we have a funeral to perform.

HARRY   *(disbelief in his voice)* What?!

BILL   Oh yes. We have to give Sid a proper send off.

HARRY   You have definitely all been down in this bunker for too long.

BILL   *(ignoring him and laying the box in the centre of the table)* Mags! Have you got the Operations Manual?

MAGS	*(grabbing it)* Yes, love.
BILL	Page seventy one. The laying to rest of comrades killed in action. Gather round everyone.
MAGS	Fancy you knowing the page.
BILL	It's something I often read, strangely enough.
HARRY	Like I said – down here too long.
	(Everyone gathers around the table – some with their backs to the audience. Meanwhile CONNOR gradually comes to – sitting up slowly and overhearing what everyone else is saying.)
MAGS	Ooh, it's ever so complicated. We're supposed to have a firing squad, casket bearers and a bugler.
BILL	Well, we can't do any of that. We'll start with passing the word. *(He declaims)* 'All hands bury the dead.'
	(CONNOR reacts with horror and checks himself all over to see if he's still alive.)
EVERYONE	All hands bury the dead.
BILL	We are gathered here to bury our comrade – fallen in action. We therefore commit his body to the deep...
PETER	*(interrupting)* ...but we're not burying him at sea...
BILL	But we will. We'll heave the box in the sea when we leave...
	(At this, CONNOR gives a yell, leaps to his feet but nearly falls over because his ankles are tied, hops over to the wall, picks up TAYLOR's abandoned gun and grabs the dress form, with the wedding dress on. Everyone looks at him.)
CONNOR	*(crazed)* You're not burying me!

HARRY	No, no, son! We're burying Sid!
CONNOR	*(momentarily taken aback)* Who's Sid?
HARRY	He came with a message and Doris killed him!
CONNOR	*(crazed again)* So now you're killing people at random are you? Well, you won't get me…you…bunch of lunatics. If you take one step towards me, this woman gets it! *(He actually looks at his 'hostage' and yells, throwing the dress form away from him)* She's got no head!! *(He raises the automatic weapon and points it at them)* Beheading people as well, now! I know your game!
HARRY	*(raising his hands and slowly advancing towards CONNOR)* Son! You've got it all wrong! Let's just sit down quietly and talk this through!
CONNOR	*(he starts gabbling)* I know what this is! I'm being tested! This is some mind-control experiment devised by the MOD! First you make me baby sit a load of teenagers for months and all they say are things like, "Whatever" and "Random", which drives me round the bend. Then you shut me up in a place with lunatic geriatrics, while one of you gives me pills to keep me awake and she *(he waves the gun at TAYLOR)* keeps knocking me out! You pretend that we're locked in here and I don't know night from day and now you're going to bury me alive until I'm broken! *(He suddenly notices BILL)* Who's the old geezer in pyjamas?
PETER	*(having a brainwave)* He's a doctor! He's going to make you better!
CONNOR	What, give me more pills! I'll kill him before I let him near me!
	(SHELTON and JOAN appear in the doorway.)

SHELTON	What's going on here? Marine! Put down that weapon! That's an order!
CONNOR	*(laughing hysterically)* A woman Commodore? You think I'm going to fall for that one? That's not even realistic! Do me a favour!
TAYLOR	*(sighing)* I suppose it's up to me, again. *(She moves towards CONNOR.)*
JOAN	Don't be silly! He's armed!
TAYLOR	It's my gun and it's not loaded.
	(CONNOR looks desperate. He tries to fire the gun at TAYLOR but it is empty. She slowly advances on him – he throws the gun away and suddenly sucks his thumb.)
CONNOR	*(sulkily)* Leave me alone or I'll tell my mum.
JOAN	That's it! He's gone completely ga-ga now! I told you that Vulcan Death Grip thing would brain damage him!
TAYLOR	*(putting her arm round CONNOR)* It's OK. He's just regressed, that's all. We covered this two weeks ago in the Interrogation Course. *(She unties his legs)* Some people regress when they're broken. He'll be fine when he's had some psychiatric care.
SHELTON	Midshipman, you'd better go outside and radio the medics. I'm afraid your Platoon Leader is going to need the men in white coats.
TAYLOR	Righto. I mean, yes, ma'am. *(She leads CONNOR to a chair and sits him down. He is still sucking his thumb.)* Now you just sit there, like a good boy. I'll be back in a minute.
CONNOR	My mummy will be here soon and she's going to take me to school.

TAYLOR	Yes of course she is. Just wait there and mummy will be here very soon. I promise.
	(TAYLOR TAYLOR retrieves her gun and exits, saluting SHELTON on the way out, which SHELTON returns.)
HARRY	This is terrible. You read about things like this going on. The State taking people away and brutalising them.
PETER	*(annoyed)* Hold up a minute! No-one's 'brutalised' anyone here. This lad is just a victim of his own neuroses. We've done nothing to him...apart from Joanie giving him a worming tablet...
SHELTON	A worming tablet?
JOAN	*(exasperated)* Look! Will everyone stop going on about the worming tablet! It was one tiny little pill, which I hoped he would think was a sedative. I've been giving them to my cats for years!
HARRY	Excuse me but your cats are completely manic! They've shredded more pairs of curtains than I've had hot dinners! And they've made your dog into a nervous wreck.
JOAN	*(concerned)* That's true. I never thought it might be the tablets.
SHELTON	*(brisk)* Well, now. I think we are losing sight of what's important. Second Officer Morris has informed me of the regrettable situation that has occurred down here. I can only apologise on behalf of the Royal Navy for allowing such a lamentable oversight...
PETER	Begging your pardon, ma'am, but will this affect our pensions?
SHELTON	No, no. Rest assured you will still get your full pensions. I

shall see to that.

MAGS   Oh, that's a relief! Thank you ma'am!

SHELTON   However, I have an interesting proposition for you.

JOAN   You're gonna love this, guys!

SHELTON   I recently received a memo from the top brass saying that since so many facilities are being decommissioned – due to the cuts excetera – they are actively welcoming any suggestions for the private sector to create tourist opportunities.

            (SHELTON looks at them all with an excited smile but they all look blank.)

BILL   Sorry, ma'am, we're not with you. How does this affect us?

SHELTON   I think I may have lost the common touch. I spend too much time dealing with jargonised paperwork. Joan – you tell them.

JOAN   Yes, ma'am. Basically, you numbskulls, the Commodore is offering us the chance to buy the bunker and turn it into a tourist attraction – a bit like the London War Rooms.

PETER   *(the penny drops)* What...you mean we would *own* this place and show people round it?

JOAN   By George, I think he's got it.

SHELTON   I really think that this place ticks all the boxes. The Ministry of Defence requires that the facility is in good order...which it obviously is...and that it is run by former service personnel who can best explain its systems.

MAGS   Ooh! I'll have to give that Operations manual a good read, now.

SHELTON   The MOD has even set aside a modest budget for training in marketing and tourism for approved projects.

PETER   That would be wonderful!

SHELTON   Of course, you would have to be able to come up with the cash to buy this place.

BILL   And how much would that be, ma'am?

SHELTON   Well, MOD guidelines for a place like this are in the order of fifty thousand pounds.

JOAN   Do you mind if we have a discussion, ma'am?

SHELTON   Not at all.

JOAN   Right, everyone! Huddle!

    (JOAN, MAGS, PETER, HARRY and BILL go into a corner in a huddle and 'discuss' things quietly. TAYLOR enters and salutes SHELTON.)

TAYLOR   The medics are here, ma'am.

SHELTON   *(returning the salute)* Carry on, midshipman.

TAYLOR   *(going over to CONNOR and speaking in a soothing voice)* Your mummy's here, now. Shall we go and see her?

    (CONNOR nods and, still sucking his thumb, he allows TAYLOR to lead him to the doorway. JOAN notices and they all pause their discussion to wave goodbye.)

HARRY   Bye, bye, son. Look after yourself.

MAGS   Yes. Take care now.

JOAN   We'll come and visit you.

CONNOR   *(suddenly terrified)* NO! *(He yells and runs off down the corridor.)*

TAYLOR   *(sighing)* Here we go again. *(She shouts)* Wait there! Or mummy will be cross! *(Then she exits.)*

SHELTON Oh dear. That poor Marine may never recover.

PETER I don't know what did it, ma'am, whether it was us or the teenagers.

SHELTON *(drily)* Trust me. I speak from personal experience...it was the teenagers. *(Changing tack.)* So...have you reached a decision?

JOAN *(stepping forward and saluting)* Yes, ma'am! On behalf of the personnel in Sea Reconnaissance bunker seventeen, we would like to accept your proposal to buy the facility and turn it into a tourist attraction.

SHELTON Excellent! There is just one proviso, however. For the sake of your pensions and my continuing career, I'm afraid I shall have to ask you to abide by the Official Secrets Act and never tell a living soul about the...er...oversight of the last twenty years. Is that agreed?

(Everyone murmurs agreement.)

Now, I've had a tour of the rest of the facility. Show me what you've managed to restore in here.

(HARRY leaps forward enthusiastically.)

HARRY I'll just switch on the sonar, ma'am. The computer, as you can see, is fully functional.

(He switches on the sonar and it begins beeping. Everyone gathers around the equipment.)

SHELTON Good Lord! What's that being picked up on sonar?

PETER Oh, don't worry ma'am. It's only a telecoms ship and mini-sub. They're laying cables out in the bay.

SHELTON   Well, that all seems jolly good. Obviously, this equipment
            will have to be disconnected from the Admiralty computers.
            Will they still function as stand alone equipment?

HARRY   Oh yes ma'am. We can have everything beeping and
            bleeping for the tourists – don't worry.

SHELTON   Jolly good. Well, I think I should go now. If you would all
            report to me at my office at o-nine-hundred on Monday, I
            think we can sort out the relevant paperwork and get this
            project underway. *(SHELTON turns to leave and then turns
            back.)* Oh, and Joanie...you and I must have dinner together
            and catch up.

JOAN   *(smiling)* Yes, ma'am!

PETER   We'll walk you to the door, ma'am.

SHELTON   If you would.

            *(Everyone exits. The lights begin to dim, very slowly. The
            sonar is still beeping. We hear a telephone ringing. Then
            Voices Offstage.)*

VOICE 1   Commodore's office.

VOICE 2   Is the Commodore there?

VOICE 1   No, she's out at the moment. Can I take a message?

VOICE 2   Yes. It's Coastal Operations here. We've had a signal from
            Communications via Sea Recon seventeen that there is
            unauthorised vessel activity in the bay nearby. Can you tell
            the Commodore that we happened to have a gunboat on
            smuggler duty up the coast and we sent it to investigate. The
            Captain's not in a very good mood and he's likely to blow
            the little buggers out of the water, if they give him any

trouble. Just thought I ought to warn you.

VOICE 1   Righto. She won't be pleased but I'll let her know.

(Everyone comes back into the room, smiling and joking. The sonar is still beeping.)

HARRY   Well, you got a right result there, didn't you?

JOAN   And for you as well, Harry. We shall be needing a maintenance man, if we get this contract, won't we?

PETER   Definitely.

BILL   Well, whatever happens, we'll still get our pensions.

MAGS   Yes. That was the most important thing.

(The beeping stops and HARRY goes to look at the sonar.)

HARRY   Hey up! That ship's disappeared off the sonar.

JOAN   Thank God! I was going to ask you to turn it off anyway. That beeping was driving me mad! *(She picks up her bag)* Well, I don't know about you lot but I'm off to the pub. It's been a hell of a day.

(They all start gathering up their stuff.)

MAGS   It certainly has! I mean I was getting to the point of thinking "What else could possibly happen today?"

(They all laugh. HARRY switches off the machines and everyone begins to exit. JOAN helps MAGS with the dress form. Before they leave, there is an announcer's voice (heard only by the audience.)

VOICE   This is the BBC news at six o'clock. A ship, laying telecoms cables, was sunk today off the Kent coast – apparently fired upon, by mistake, by a Royal Navy gunboat. Fortunately,

there were no casualties *(the voice starts fading)*. A
spokesman for the Royal Navy said......

BLACKOUT.

MUSIC.

THE END.

FURNITURE LIST

Throughout: Operations console(see set plan), one square table(with one leg shorter than the others), four wooden or plastic chairs, two typist's chairs. Coat/hat stand, possibly a metal cupboard. Red light.

Set dressing: Admiralty wall chart, posters. Possibly a rota/year planner.

PROPERTY LIST

Throughout:	Operations Manual (thick book, under table leg), telephone book, three battery operated storm lamps, sonar manual (under operations console), Day Book and pen, Scrabble set.
Page 1:	blindfold, mobile phone(with camera facility) in pocket (HARRY) toolbox (with torch, screwdriver and wire cutters in), Official Secrets Act papers (PETER)
Page 3:	pint of milk, handbag (containing worming pills, rubber gloves, cleaning spray), bunch of keys (JOAN)
Page 8:	small or tight Petty Officer's uniform (notebook in jacket pocket) (PETER)
Page 10:	large dress form (dressed in a wedding dress), sewing things in shoulder bag, bunch of keys with dog tags (MAGS)
Page 12:	roll of electrical wire (HARRY)
Page 18:	tray of tea and biscuits (JOAN)
Page 23:	toolbox (HARRY)
Page 25:	mug of coffee (JOAN)
Page 29:	HARRY takes a photo with his mobile phone, JOAN exits with storm lamp.
Page 30:	JOAN exits again with a storm lamp.
Page 32:	tray of tea and biscuits (JOAN)
Page 35:	HARRY gets notebook from PETER's jacket pocket.
Page 37:	JOAN gives HARRY a bunch of keys.
Page 38:	automatic weapons (TAYLOR and CONNOR)
Page 42:	MAGS removes tray of tea things.
Page 43:	MAGS returns with tray of tea things.

LIGHTING AND EFFECTS PLOT

NOTE TO TECHNICAL CREW: For this set, apart from general
lighting, you will need lights in the corridor at the back of the set, an
orange bulb and a blue bulb inside the 'console' on stage, plus a red bulb
that flashes on and off. Other lighting (from the storm lamps) is
controlled by the actors.

Start of play: *BLACKOUT. MUSIC. Then shaft of light from open
door. PETER 'switches lights on'. LIGHTS to general
interior level.*

Page 19   CUE: MAGS: "Good natured and all."

LIGHTS : Blackout. Stage lit by storm lamps.

Page 20:   CUE: HARRY: "Do you want to put the power back on,
Pete?"

*LIGHTS: Up to general interior. Orange light from
sonar. Red light in corner is flashing. MAGS switches off
storm lamps.*

SFX: Sonar blips.

Page 21:   CUE: MAGS: "switching off sonar now."

SFX : sonar blips stop.

CUE: HARRY: "Righto."

*LIGHTS: HARRY 'switches off lights.' Red light is still
flashing.*

SFX : Recorded telephone ringing and conversation.

CUE: VOICE 2: "Yes, ma'am. Will do."

SFX: Red light goes out. Stage blackout.

Page 23:   *LIGHTS: Blackout. Then shaft of light from open
doorway. MAGS 'switches on lights'. Lights to general
interior level.*

Page 28:	CUE: HARRY: "The Chairman joined the police force."
	LIGHTS : JOAN switches on all the storm lamps.
Page 29:	CUE: PETER: "...or I really will kill you."
	LIGHTS: Blackout. Stage is lit by storm lamps.
Page 30:	CUE: MAGS: "Just be patient."
	LIGHTS: Up to general interior setting. JOAN re-enters and switches off the storm lamps.
Page 31:	CUE: HARRY: "This computer is booting up."
	LIGHTS: Blue light coming from 'computer'.
Page 38:	CUE: JOAN: (Screams) "Oh my God!"
	LIGHTS: Blackout.
	SFX: Recorded telephone ringing and conversation.
Page 39:	CUE: VOICE 2: "Will do."
	LIGHTS: Up to general interior setting.
Page 48:	CUE: JOAN: "I know what the next step is! It's...it's..."
	LIGHTS: lights start flashing slowly.
	SFX: Klaxon interspersed with voice effect.
	LIGHTS : Eventual blackout. Actors switch on storm lamps.
Page 53:	CUE: MAGS: "Whatever is our Carol going to do, without a wedding dress?"
	LIGHTS: Actors must simultaneously switch off storm lamps.
Page 54:	*SFX: MUSIC.*
	LIGHTS: Blackout.
	SFX: Recorded telephone ringing and conversation.
Page 55:	CUE: VOICE 1: "Yes, ma'am."
	LIGHTS: Actors switch on storm lamps.

Page 62:   CUE: JOAN: "I appreciate the gesture, OK?"

SFX: *Faint sound of tapping on metal.*

Page 67:   CUE: *(CONNOR screaming and clutching a butter knife goes running past the open door...)*

SFX: *Distant shouting and banging on metal door.*

Page 69:   CUE: *(BILL appears in the doorway...)*

LIGHTS: *Up to general interior setting.*

CUE: PETER "Oh, it's been terrible!"

LIGHTS: PETER *switches off storm lamps.*

Page 82:   CUE: HARRY: "The computer, as you can see, is fully functional."

SFX: *Sonar blips.*

Page 83:   CUE: SHELTON: "If you would."

LIGHTS: *Begin to dim very slowly.*

SFX: *Recorded telephone ringing and conversation.*

Page 84:   CUE: MAGS: "Yes. That was the most important thing."

SFX : *Sonar blip stops.*

CUE: MAGS: "What else could possibly happen today?"

LIGHTS : *Continue to dim.*

SFX: *Recorded BBC announcement, which fades.*

Page 85:   LIGHTS: *Blackout.*

SFX: *Music.*

CURTAIN CALLS.

SUGGESTED SET PLAN FOR BUNKERED

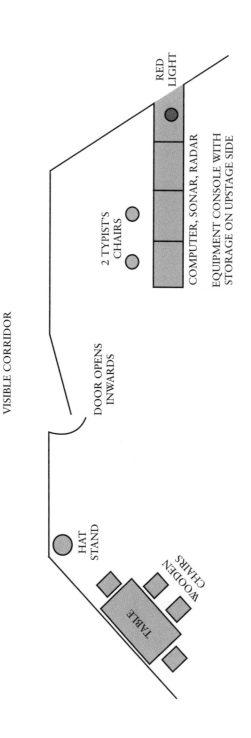

VISIBLE CORRIDOR

RED LIGHT

2 TYPIST'S CHAIRS

COMPUTER, SONAR, RADAR

EQUIPMENT CONSOLE WITH STORAGE ON UPSTAGE SIDE

DOOR OPENS INWARDS

HAT STAND

WOODEN CHAIRS

TABLE

BUNKERED EQUIPMENT CONSOLE

AUDIENCE VIEW

PLAIN GREY OR BLACK
COMPUTER/SONAR HOUSING

PLAIN GREY OR BLACK STORAGE
UNITS/WORKBENCHES

RED
LIGHT

STAGE LEFT 'WALL'

ACTOR'S VIEW

STAGE LEFT 'WALL'

RED
LIGHT

ORANGE
LIGHT

BLUE
LIGHT

DAYBOOK MANUAL

STORM
LAMPS

SCRABBLE

The Diefenbunker in Canada's Cold War Museum which gives an idea of the style and type of equipment and furniture used in the Cold war period.